Faith in the In-Between

Trusting God while the story is still unfolding

Author Diana Allen

Copyright

Faith in the In-Between:

Trusting God while the story is still unfolding

Publishing Assistance – Dr. Nina Addison

www.drninaaddison.com

info@drninaaddison.com

Graphics and Marketing: Dominique Jimerson

Dominique_jimerson@yahoo.com

ISBN: 979-8-9864595-4-7

This Book Belongs To

___

Acknowledgements:

I want to thank my Lord and Savior, Jesus Christ, for choosing to save me and for inspiring me to do what he purposed in my life.

I truly thank my three lovelies for their continued support and for making me feel like I can do anything.

Thank you, Felica, for being a confidante in this season of my life. I thank everyone for your thoughts and prayers.

Table of Contents

Introduction

Greater is he that is in me than he that is in the world, 1 John 4:4.

Hello and welcome to a sneak peek of my journey of becoming who God says I am. Yes, this is a Christian-based book, but don't turn away from it because it just might be what you need to start your own journey of becoming...

My journey through the storm, how do I begin talking about something that affected every part of my being? My mind, my body, my spirit. This is a brief look into my mind, the words I have written down as I experienced the troubles that interrupted my life. Four months was only the beginning of what seemed like a lifetime when you are going through; it doesn't have an end. This is a particular time in my life when things begin to fall apart. It was the beginning of my becoming, and yet not so, because God has been transforming me for a very long time; I just didn't know it. This is after my late husband passed. I was trying to figure out how I should manage things moving forward. I wanted to be okay financially. I tried my hand at investing; it went well, so I tried more. The money grew. When it was time to take it out, I couldn't without putting more money into it, so I did. It was a rolling cycle of trying to get my money back, only to hit a wall, until I had no more to give.

I tried very hard to make it right, but I couldn't; my money is stuck, and I don't have access to it. I was in disbelief, I was hurting, it blew my mind, God was not in this at all, I didn't consult him, I was making moves on my own. That's when I gave the enemy the opportunity; he needed to disrupt my life even more. And he did, he was shooting those fiery darts at me. I was panicking, Lord, please help me! I was begging and pleading for this to turn around. I felt like I was in a nightmare. The worst part is that I couldn't tell anyone, I was embarrassed, I was ashamed, and I was afraid; I had to suffer alone. I didn't know that the enemy wanted me in that position so that I wouldn't rise. My children had no idea why I was seeking God the way I was. I had gone into a dark place; my life was spinning out of control. No one knew my turmoil. I am hurting, Lord; everything is happening to me right after the other. It is just hitting me so hard. It's a terrible storm, tossing me every which way. My mind is not clear. I feel so defeated. What am I supposed to do? How can I get out of this? I keep praying and asking you, Lord, to rescue me, but nothing is happening. I can't move. Every time I try to fix it, it's worse. Please help me. Why aren't you answering me?

One day, I had a dream, and I started seeking God to understand it. As I sought, I learned more about him. He was talking to me in different ways, in dreams, songs, and sermons. I wasn't listening before, but God has a way of getting our attention. Lord, I don't understand what you are trying to tell me in scripture. I read it, but I don't understand how this applies to my life now. I need you to speak to my situation specifically. What I remember the most is how God spoke to me in song. I was in a listening posture. I remember waking up at 2-3 o'clock in the morning in despair, wondering how and why this happened to me, and when I say you can just walk into a storm, my goodness, it just comes out of nowhere. I didn't even see it coming. I was looking around like…is this really happening to me? And that storm answered…yes, it is, now hold on tight cause it's going to be a doozy! And boy was I being tossed. I didn't know one day from another. I was in a fog; I couldn't see straight. I didn't let it be visible to others; you couldn't tell that anything was wrong because I still walked around in conversation with people, went through the daily motions of life, but was literally in turmoil every day. Can you imagine? I'm crying, I'm praying, I'm angry, I'm praying, I'm sad, I'm praying. I didn't stop praying because I realized I was in a test and needed something to hold on to.

As I went through this journey, I noticed that the songs I listened to changed as I grew stronger. It went from asking God to get me out of this, to thanking him for going through it with me, to claiming victory, to God getting the glory, and victory is won. Those songs were my inspiration; I clung to every one of them. My Pastor Allen and the Bishop I watched online were on the same page with their messages, which gave me hope, because in this storm, I had gotten so weak. Every time it seemed as if I had a breakthrough, the devil came in to distract me with more trouble, and again, things fell apart because I allowed what I was going through to distract me from focusing on God. We must recognize that Satan doesn't want us to have what God has for us and doesn't want us to trust God, so he will try with every chance he gets to cause us to fall, fail, and be defeated. He wants us to give up. I was listening to an online Bible class I had started because one of my friends had sent me a sermon to listen to daily. I had to be surrounded by God's word, reading, hearing, listening, and meditating on his word, because I need him. I need his strength to survive. I thank God for the foundation he placed in my life through my parents; they planted the seed that showed me who I needed and how to get to him. See, God will put people in your life to direct you and to guide you. Destiny helpers, thank God for mine.

Satan was trying hard to get me to stop trusting God. Every time doubt came into my head, every time something failed, I quoted the scripture, "though you slay me, yet will I trust you" (Job 13:15). God was silent. He was not answering me, I didn't see any miracle moves, any dramatic or drastic changes, no heavens opening or Jesus coming down to save me. None of that! I kept hearing the song "God provides," and I had to realize, after months of disappointment, that God is providing. Nothing in my household has changed. We still have a roof over our heads, still eat every day, still have clothes and vehicles, bills paid on time, a paycheck still coming in, no sickness, nothing unfortunate. God provides! And I am very grateful, with my ungrateful self, because guess what? I was still in that storm and wanted OUT! Because I felt that if I didn't get out, I could be in a predicament where I had no home, vehicle, or living paycheck to paycheck. That thinking was from the enemy. I know, "I've never seen the righteous forsaken nor his seed begging for bread" Psalm 37:25. But, those words were not in the front of my mind. All I could see was my situation, the chaos right now. And I needed my right now God to deliver me from this storm. Satan has tried several times to take my life, but God said No! Satan couldn't get my physical body, so he tried to get my mind, and when I tell you my mind was in a dark space, yes, the enemy wanted me to end my life! That thought was in and out so quickly! Everything flashed in my thoughts, my salvation, my children, my family, NO! Though I was still in a state of despair, my emotions were up and down, because I was in warfare, and the devil was trying so hard to get me. It was after another failed attempt to get out of my situation that my whole being gave up, and to be honest, I questioned my belief. I asked for forgiveness later.

I came home and just cried. I was shaking, I didn't know what to do, I couldn't sit still, I was rocking and crying and asking God for help and not to leave me alone. Because I felt so alone. I remember being at home alone, I remember feeling so defeated, I didn't want to do anything but somehow, I remembered that I am more than a conqueror through Christ Jesus. I went into praise-and-worship mode. I played some spiritual music that uplifted me. See, we must praise

God no matter how we feel, no matter what we are going through, because he is still God who is Sovereign, and I tell you all, suddenly I had this peace, his comfort, and I knew that he is working it out for me. I went to sleep that night and didn't wake up until the morning. I slept well. I was so at peace that I started practicing the praise dance that I was going to teach the youth at my church. I was listening to the words from the song "Speak the name," and I just burst out in tears. My son came over to me, and I tried to give a testimony through my tears. See, even though I was still in my storm, God continues to reign in my life; his name is power, and he is in control.

Can you imagine not having God while you go through something? That could be the reason why suicide rates are high; we need God. God cares, and he is working it out for our good. I now realize that I wasn't alone, because when you are in a storm, your mind is not thinking clearly, you are in a weak state of mind, and Satan will take advantage of your weakness. But "no weapon formed against me shall prosper", Isaiah 54:17. God has my back, and when my Heavenly Father is around, he is power backing me up. God will give you what you need, and I needed his words to comfort me. One day, a young lady came by my house to sell those solar windows. While she was trying to talk to me, a bumblebee attacked her, and I thought," Okay, she will leave now. Nope, the bee left, and she returned. When she did, the bee returned; this happened about three times.

During that time, my son called to say he was ready to be picked up from school. So now I am thinking, "man, I've got to get past their fight to get to my truck." I ran to my truck, and she followed me. I told her that I had so much going on that I couldn't add anything else to my plate. You know what she did? She started talking about the goodness of the Lord, quoting scriptures on how to fight Satan and standing strong against him through the word of God. You know what I was thinking? I need that, I need to quote those scriptures, and I know that I needed to intentionally do this. I was a little jealous of how easily she brought that out. She encouraged her sister in Christ during her time of need. She was determined not to let distractions deter her from the message God gave her to share with me. I want to do that; I want to encourage others in their time of need. I downloaded Bible commentaries and devotional readings and study them to understand. I put my eyes on the prize of Jesus Christ and was less focused on the worries that were concerning me. I learned how to take each day in prayer and not worry about the future. So yes, some of the things that I was going through were broken off when God had me where he wanted me, humbly submitting to him. Trusting and believing that he will bring me through this. It was so hard, so long. My back was literally against the wall. I had no way out. I had to trust him or fall. That was it. Though he slays me, yet will I trust him, that was my mantra daily.

Trusting was very difficult; it is an action word because that was me putting my all into it, literally allowing God to transform the way I was thinking and doing those things that are pleasing to him. It's not standing still; we are moving in the direction of the Lord when we trust him. God is my everything; He is absolute power. He can do anything. The impossible, he will move mountains. I know that at his appointed time, he will deliver me from my situation. Until then, he keeps me steady when I am focused on him. He does all of this while comforting me through the pain that I am experiencing to make it easier for me to endure. He gives me peace while he is working behind the scenes. "I will bless the Lord at all times, and his praise shall continually be in my mouth," Psalm 34. God has given me breakthroughs, and I am so grateful to him because they give me relief; the pressure is too much at times. However, the relief is brief. The minute I think that I am free from all of this, the devil is after me again, but I guess he never stopped; he was just waiting. I won't give up because I have too much to lose. I can do all things through Christ who strengthens me. God knows how much I can bear, but being honest, I don't think I am as strong as he thinks I am.

I don't know how I am feeling right now. I know disbelief is one of them, not in God, who does all things; it's the disbelief that the attacks keep coming even after I have overcome something. When does it stop? I guess I am a little angry, not at God, but at Satan, because he keeps bothering me, and I guess I am tired of having to be strong repeatedly. He won't make me curse God. I refuse to be defeated. It just makes me seek God more, and you know what? That's not weakness at all; that is resilience. God will rescue me. There was a feeling in me that kind of let me know that it wasn't over, that I had more to go. I will continue to trust God with my whole heart, mind, and spirit. I am fasting today, and I'm learning how to trust beyond knowing what I think should happen or what I am seeing. God has not forgotten me; he knows where I am, and he will deliver me in time. One thing we need to be aware of is that God is in everything, and why wouldn't he be in our everyday life and in every situation? Even when we get ourselves caught up in those situations. He will help us get out of it, but not by snapping his fingers. We will most definitely know the consequences of our actions as he lovingly brings us out of our struggles.

Confusion is what I am feeling right now. God is not the author of confusion. I don't know what God wants me to do. I know that Satan is trying to shake me up, but I won't make a move until God shows me his face. I am trying to listen; the Holy Spirit will guide me. I lay in bed at night, talking to God and asking what he wants from me. I am not afraid, I am not so anxious, but I am anticipating something happening. Have you ever gotten that feeling? It's like every fiber in your being is on alert. I'm looking everywhere for my miracle, my blessing, my favor. I don't know how it will come, but I know it will come, and it will come on time because I know that God loves me and will supply my every need, and he does not lie. He keeps his promises. So, I asked God for a sign to let me know if he wanted me to go a certain way. He showed me the way; now I must believe that he will have another ram in the bush for me. I only have a week, one week before all hell breaks loose. But I am a believer in all things God. He will do the impossible, and the devil will be defeated once again. God is Almighty God! No one can out-power, outsource, or outdo God! He is Absolute. I guess Satan knows this already, so he tries to come through us to thwart God, but this temple belongs to my one and only true and living God. I trust him always. So, I continue to read and study his words for my power and strength. I know that God has great things in store for me.

I have been fasting and praying for a week. I have been reading the bible for an understanding. This is an experience, scriptures that I thought I knew, I'm getting another understanding. I'm letting myself open to God guiding me. And every time I feel strong, here comes Satan tossing in some doubt! The thing about not knowing what God is going to do is that you don't know, so you start guessing and leaning to your own understanding. We make moves that may not be what God wants us to do. It's hard listening when you have distractions everywhere, at home, at work, at church. We don't know how to handle distractions, but God does. He will get rid of them so that we can concentrate on him. Our decisions need to be confirmed by God; we need to wait on him before we make any moves, otherwise we could repeat the same mistakes. So, God removed my present distractions, and I was able to hear and allow the Holy Spirit to have his way.

The thing with the distractions is that the troubles keep coming back. I need strength, Lord. I must learn how to recognize them when they come. I need to respond appropriately and not panic. So, I got on my knees in prayer and then went into worship with the Lord. I feel your peace. I am learning about your character. God will bring us to our knees until there is no one else but him that you lean and depend on. That's where I am now. No one can help me but God. When I come out of this, I will know without a doubt that it is God. The waiting is so hard because deadlines are still set, but I'm still doing my part, and don't think that old enemy is not trying to sabotage me every step of the way. I have weak moments where I just want to give up and not think about my situation, but God reminds me who he is. He is God Almighty, and I will continue to trust him. I am praying, praising, and worshiping God daily. I'm getting stronger in faith, which is why that devil finds a new way to cause trouble in my life. I feel some type of way, when I feel God's silence, the not knowing is one of the toughest experiences for me. Blessed are those who believe and do not see. I believe in God and is his word. I am comforted because he honors his words. If he said it, then I believe it, and you sometimes need a reminder before you go crazy. Satan will get into your thoughts, and all kinds of scenarios occur. God is not the author of confusion; he will not have us confused about our purpose. So, we must listen and follow his lead. Pray constantly. He knows what I am going through.

I know that he has a plan for my life. I must trust him completely to take care of me. He won't let me fall. I have my ups and downs in this faith walk; it has been tough, especially with Satan putting obstacles in my way at every turn. I am persevering. I call on Jesus and the Holy Spirit for my strength and power. I have begged God and pleaded with him to get me out of this situation. It has been ugly some nights. I was on the floor crying like a baby one night. I thought it was over, and got bad news that it wasn't. That shook my faith a little. I was again questioning, angry, and doubting. Then I was ashamed because how can I be shaken so easily when I know Satan is trying his hardest to get me to curse God and die. I got myself up off the floor, put on some praise and worship music, and pressed through the pain. I listened to the words because those people have gone through what I am going through, and their testimony is helping me to have the strength to keep going. God is near to me; I learned that during my study. He won't leave me nor forsake me. I need to pass this test so that I can make him smile and be proud of me. I want him to be pleased with me. I am determined to follow God. The devil will be defeated! He is defeated!

Break Loose

It's breaking
The hold is not so tight
It has been such a long journey
It has been a fight
Not physically, boxing gloves are not adorned
It's a spiritual fight; your whole armor must be worn
It's breaking loose
It's breaking free
It must be broken from the enemy
Stuck in the middle
Can't go forward, don't want to return
To a life of regrets, because lessons learned
Fatigue surrounds me
Mind, body, and soul
Get up, to press forward
Dare to be bold
Declare your freedom
From the one who is sin
Through our Lord Jesus Christ
The one who always wins
Break loose, break free
From generations bound
Defeat, defeat is not the sound,

That you hear from chains dropping to the ground
Glorious days are ahead
Dark clouds dissipated
Sunny days anticipated
Breaking loose from the dark corners of the mind
Freedom from the proverbial ties that bind
It's breaking
So, relax, relate, and receive.

The journey of becoming is a process; we don't go from one point in our life to another without the journey of getting there, the in-between. Most people don't see the road you have traveled, the trials and tribulations, the burdens, the frustrations, the anxiety, or the lack. The only thing some will see is that you have reached the promised land. They won't understand what you have surrendered to the process; they won't understand how God was with you in the process or how he carried you through it. They won't understand that the process should not be avoided, hated, or discouraged, but should be embraced because we must go through it to get to the promise. For example, when you are searching for a new job, whether for security, prosperity, financial increase, or a need, you go through the process of looking for jobs in your field; the pay rate, the location, the benefits; then, when you find one, you look at the description to see if it is a fit, so you apply for the position. In the meantime, you may be going through it at your present job, or at home, about to lose it for lack of income. You are praying for it to reach the person it needs to reach; you get a phone call for an interview; you prepare for the interview or two, stressing about what you will say or how you will say it; then you pray again, and finally you get a call stating you got the job! No one knows what you went through to get that job but you and God, because you brought him into it with you. All anyone will see is that God blessed you with more, not the process of getting you there.

Everyone has their own road to travel; let us be mindful that the decisions we make on that road won't always be the popular choice, but if we are allowed another day in life, we can always learn to make better choices.
I want to add this disclaimer. Matthew 7:1-3 talks about not judging others unless you want to be judged. This means that if you judge others for what they have done in life, you will be judged by the same standards by our Heavenly Father. Remember, no one is perfect, no matter how you may perceive them. Christianity does not make you perfect, but we must strive for it because our Heavenly Father requires it. It doesn't mean you won't lie or make mistakes; however, as you grow in Christ, mind, body, and spirit, you don't continue in that foolishness or make a habit of it. Our God is loving, but he is a Just and Righteous God. Do you remember King David in the Bible? He was the apple of God's eye, yet he still sinned against God. He was not perfect, but his heart was turned toward God in humility, repentance, and love. God chose him for great things because of his heart, not because of his perfection.

The journeys of life are like a roller coaster, and you must hold on tight to keep your faith. Picture this. When you are in the dead of winter, and the wind is blowing so hard it almost takes your breath away, it's as if it's trying to strip your clothes from your body. You're gripping them hard to keep in the warmth of that inner glow, but it's a struggle. The cold winds are not letting up. You're trying hard not to let go because you know that once you let go, that covering is gone, and you are bare, at the mercy of the elements. You wonder why the winds are going against you so hard? Then you see him, the enemy, a wolf in sheep's clothing, blowing down everything we hold dear, trying to strip us bare so that we have nothing to hold on to. He doesn't let up until God shines his light on us and gives us peace when we call his name. That's the roller coaster, the ups and downs, the enemy's attack, and God is that warmth, the inner glow, the peace. He is our shelter. So, bundle up and hold on tight to God's unchanging hands. Hold on to his word, which is the Holy Bible.

Chapter 1 - A Test

The surprise of my life was when I found out that God himself would take me through a storm, a test, and here I was rebuking the devil for everything that was happening to me, because that's what I grew up on, that's what I heard people say all the time. Whenever something bad happened, the first thing out of the mouth was, "I rebuke you, Satan!" and when I found out that my Lord was taking me through some things, I had to pause; not my loving Father, he would not do this to me. Well, yes, he will, and he did, but only to get me back on the right track. I never did like receiving a spanking; I always tried to learn my lessons quickly so I wouldn't have to endure the consequences of disobedience for long. However, it took me quite a few attempts to get it right. I was struggling; surrender was hard.

I was giving up the reins and allowing God to be in control of something I thought I could handle on my own. God allows things to happen in our lives to build us up in strength because life can take us off course and cause destruction that weakens us. We have work to do for the Kingdom of God. Now I'm not saying the devil won't stir up the pot with his antics, because he does. Remember Job, when God allowed Satan to test him? He will make the situation seem worse than it is, only to get your mind off the Lord and to curse God. (Please do not do that.) Have y'all heard that saying, "Seeing is believing?" Well, what I saw almost took me out. It was happening in real time. But the hype is not what you think. What I mean is, for example, among everything I was already battling, I received my mortgage bill, and it was doubled. Right away, I was on the phone trying to find out why the bill was so large. I am telling you, these companies need a better system of doing things, because over the course of three months, yes, that's how long it took me to get things straightened out. I talked to multiple people who didn't have the same information, didn't ask the same questions, and didn't have the same resolution. The only thing they told me that was the same was to call back in about two weeks to see if what they did changed anything.

At this time, I haven't paid my mortgage because it was too high and kept rising each month. So, do you know what I had to do to solve it? I submitted and cried out to my Lord. I finally put it in his hands. I prayed for favor, to get someone who would help me with my situation. (Of course, God can put money in my bank account, or just make it disappear, but he will also use people to do his will. All of them are miracles) When I called again, I finally got someone who reviewed my file and took the time to explain what I needed. They let me know that I had to update my tax information because my husband had passed the previous year, and the information had expired. That simple. That's what I mean by hype not being what you think. Satan exacerbates the situation, and if we give up too soon or let the distraction lead us to act impulsively, we can make it worse. Believe me, my mind was racing with things to do to get out of it, sell the house, which was at the top (and that would have been bad because God blessed us with the house, and the enemy knew it. He tries to make a liar out of God).

I had to really seek the Lord because I was in panic mode, and he came through. I want to say that seeking God should be the first thing we think of, but Satan will throw us off with his antics so fast that we just react, which is not good. We must slow down, take a step back, and consult the Lord before doing anything. I got tired of the pressure, of the darts being shot my way, and you know your mind can really take you to some crazy places if you let it. Don't. Stay focused on the Source, who is God. If he brings you to it, he'll bring you through it. Surrender. He's got you. So, here's some encouragement to try God first. He won't fail you. He will comfort you during your lowest points. He did that for me. I was crying one night because things were so tough. I was upset with God because he wasn't stopping my pain. I curled up in my bed and didn't want to pray. I just cried until I fell asleep.

The next day, my friend called me that morning to say that the Lord woke her up at three in the morning, he said my name, showed her a vision of a lady in bed, lying on her side, crying. He wanted her to pray for me, and she did. I was amazed because, even though I was acting like a child, God was still comforting me through a friend's prayer. He let me know that he will not leave me nor forsake me. This is what God does. What he gave me was peace and the strength to keep going.

Chapter 2 - Don't Be Afraid

` Don't be afraid of stepping into your destiny, the thing that God has planned for you; fear will steal it. The next thing you know, you are wondering what happened to the future that God said you would have. What happened to the level up, right? Well, it's a process for sure, and we must be strong and courageous as we go through it because it can be a doozy. One day at a time, one step at a time, and trusting God for guidance will take you to your destiny.

Don't allow fear to make you stop; you may miss what God has for you if you don't continue the journey. We need to stay the course that God has mapped out for us. When we cross over into the promised land, new challenges await, and we must have the strength to overcome adversity. Stop the chatter of the naysayers. I want you to remember this: only you know what God has spoken to you; you can't explain it to others because they won't understand. Stop trying to validate what you are experiencing to make everyone else comfortable. We can allow people to steer us in the wrong direction, or we can go on our own. What I mean is, you can connect yourself to the wrong people, people who are holding you down or back and taking you in directions that God has not ordained for you. You are already afraid of what you don't see, so you may latch on to unnecessary connections or familiar connections that you are comfortable with and just stay there. You know the type of people they are, the secret haters of your life, but you can't walk away, can you?

Maybe you don't think you deserve to have better in your life, or maybe it's the fear of the unknown. Maybe you just don't want any part of the process because it's not as easy as it looks on the other person. We can make so many mistakes because we are afraid to take chances on God. We are brave when we bet on ourselves or others, but the realness of trusting God and letting go of the reins and allowing him to take control of our lives; it's scary, but we can't allow fear to control our destiny. I don't want to miss anything that God has for me. Satan is on my trail, but I will persevere.

What we must remember is that the devil is always going to try to stop the purpose, the calling that God has on our lives. Don't be afraid, be mad at the idea that the enemy is trying to stop the blessings that the Lord has for you. Also, know that we ourselves can hinder God's blessings. How, do you ask? Complaining about everything, just for the sake of complaining. Not being satisfied with anything or being very unappreciative of the life you have. Negativity is your surplus. You know what the sad part is? It is such an intricate part of your life that you go unnoticed by it. That is not the heart that God wants us to have. He doesn't want anything that looks like the heart of the enemy. Negative attitudes, disagreement with everything, and never being happy about life are just sad. Then envy and jealousy are invited in to harden the heart against others who have decided to let God change their character and receive the blessings of the Lord. Don't be disillusioned, these negative characteristics are bondage from the enemy; there is freedom in Jesus Christ. Don't allow the enemy to beat you out of your blessings, because nobody can beat God's giving. The devil will make you think he can. Yes, he can gift you, but ask yourself if you truly want it. Don't be fooled by his trickery. Faith over fear. Follow the process, it is to make you stronger.

No Fear

Why are you afraid to take the steps?
Knowing that His promises He has kept.
Why consume your thoughts with such doubt?
When you are assured that He will bring you out.
Don't take your focus off the One,
Have no fear
Close your eyes, meditate
So, you can hear.
The clear directions He is taking you
To a season of beginnings that are new.
You are the one He chose for the task,
You only have to sit back, stand on the promises, and bask,
In the favor of the Lord
As He guides you to complete
Everything before you, every need, He will meet.
Trust in the One whose limits know no bounds
Our Lord and Savior, whose truth is sound.
His word is clear,
Open your eyes to see,
Focus on the One, who is near
Then you will know
To have no fear.

Chapter 3 - Represent Christ

I remember when I was a young girl, and my mom taught us about the Lord and how we should not be ashamed of telling people that we are children of God. Growing up in the churchy scene was hard because we wanted friends, right? We wanted to be cool. We didn't want to be called bible freaks. That's why some people love the Lord in silence, in their homes, in the church, where you are free to worship without guilt. You know those instances where you might be at a concert or a similar venue, and the person at the Mic might say something about the Lord; do you say amen, in agreement, and then look around to see who saw you? Let me tell you, people will try to shame you about your belief in Christ. Don't let them.

Matthew 10:33 says, *"But whoever denies me before men, I will also deny him before my Father who is in heaven"*. I don't know about you, but I am not trying to get denied my place in heaven. The world is not worth my eternal life. Christian life is not as bad as most people believe it to be. People make it hard with the unnecessary expectations of Christianity. Don't get me wrong, sinning is still not an option, but when you start following the Lord, you won't even miss the partying and everything that goes along with it (remember Lot's wife, whose heart was turned towards Sodom and Gomorrah and not towards the Lord? Pillar of salt was her lot in life).

Side note, when I say partying, I mean just that, and you know what that's about. I don't mean enjoying dancing and having clean fun because we are Christian right? I do love to dance, and I love songs that are just good, no matter the genre. Now I just dance for the Lord when I can and sing in the choir. But so that I won't offend anyone, I only dance the dances that I grew up on or sing around family and close friends, unless I'm at a wedding or something fun, you might catch me dancing.

So anyway, your mind will be occupied with getting to know the Lord more, and believe me, once you are in his presence, there is nothing else like it. You want to know why it feels good to be in his presence? We can't have all that sin on us when we are near him, so he has started that process of shedding the unwanted habits, people, thinking, etc., bringing us towards holiness. I have so much peace when I am in his presence, and I try to be there often. I can feel when I am going astray, when I am being distracted by mundane things in life. At those times, I feel as though something is missing; I feel a distance between God and me. Something doesn't feel right. Focus is off God, the enemy is attacking, so guess what? I start to listen and watch because God is trying to get my attention. I would hear a word from a sermon as if God is speaking to me, and I realize what I was missing, my closeness with the Lord. I ask for forgiveness and get back on track with him.

You see, it's intentional and consistent; we must walk the walk and talk the talk. We may fall, but don't stay in the fallen position; we must get back up. People are watching, and you don't want to cause others to falter in their belief. When they are trying to follow the Lord, you may confuse them in their journey. Don't miss an opportunity to lead someone to Christ. The minute you profess Christianity; all eyes are on you.

Christians are judged no matter what we do; we can't enjoy life on earth, not even the simplest one, because the world has placed us in a box, like they have the Lord, and they are ready to point out any flaws to justify their own lives. Jesus came that we might have an abundant life; it doesn't mean a sinful life; people at their worst can be changed by

God. Don't judge; your own life should be reflecting that of Christ. So that others see what God sees in you.

Chapter 4 - Not Easily Persuaded

I was watching a YouTube video on how to defend your faith in any scenario. The guy was showing an old video about a beauty pageant contestant who was asked a question about gay marriages, and basically, if she had answered the question the way they wanted her to, she would have won the pageant. She answered the way God wanted her to answer and lost. But did she really lose? We think having worldly gain is a winner, but at what cost? Your soul? That gave me something to ponder. What will you do to fit into your friends' group that doesn't worship our Lord? What about at work, when you can say anything except the name of Jesus, or you offend someone playing your gospel music, do you decrease so the enemy can increase? People are very fickle, yes, they are, they will invite you to a club, a bar, knowing that you are walking with the Lord, (to note, it's nothing wrong with going, that's not the sin, so be wise and remember "birds of a feather flock together" someone quoted that) when you go for a little while to enjoy their company and leave, they get offended because you didn't stay. Hello! I just came to celebrate you for a bit, not to do what you do.

But here’s the kicker, the minute you invite them to church with you, they don’t even step foot in the door, not even for 30 minutes. It shouldn’t be a hardship to give a little time to the one who created us, but unfortunately, that is the case for most people; however, you will find that our Lord does not give up on his children, he chases after us. Which leads me to my testimonies, my journey of becoming. Everyone has a testimony about circumstances that will encourage others going through similar situations. I pray you will find the courage to let the Lord become the center of your life and feel the gentle call inviting you to let him write your story, too.

Chapter 5 - Bad Habits

My journey began when I said yes, yes in my spirit, yes in my mind, yes in my obedience to my Lord. What I mean is that my "Yes" led to my obedience, my obedience led me to my time in the wilderness, where God pruned me, strengthened me, and transformed me. I am by no means perfect, because I know that I fall and fail God. I thank God that his light guides me and orders my steps wherever I need to go. He knows exactly where I need to be. His words are a lamp unto my feet and a light unto my path, Psalm 119:105. I will follow him even when I am afraid. My focus is on him; I must keep my eyes looking straight at him and not at the enemy's attack on my life. That's a distraction to make me feel afraid, to make me unsure and inadequate, to make me doubt my God who told me to cast my cares upon him, who told me to trust in him, and not to worry. We get off balance, don't we?

Sometimes those darts hit the right spot, my God, does it send us off. The key is to recognize that it is an enemy's attack on us. Sometimes we don't recognize his attack until it is too late. We have already spiraled, the hurt and pain, the confusion has taken place in our lives. That's why we must stay vigilant and prayerful, but that's not easy when we are already in it, right? Better late than never. Know that we can't fight Satan physically; we will lose. We must fight him spiritually. (I want to reiterate that not all bad things happening to us are from the devil; there are times when God allows things to occur in our lives for our strengthening, to transform us by getting rid of things and people out of our lives that hinder us from a close relationship with God; these are tests, every one of God's children will have them. I pray for your strength to pass the test.) We must pray earnestly. When I talk about prayer, I don't think it has to be eloquent and full of righteous words; it can be simple and from the heart, but as you grow in Christ, your prayers should become stronger.

Also, you must go on a fast. What does that look like? You can fast from food, but remember, it is a spiritual fast, not a weight-loss fast. You can also fast from TV or anything that takes up your headspace and your time. Pray and ask God when to fast and what to fast from. When you do this, you empty yourself so the Holy Spirit can come in and dwell with you. Stay focused on the Lord and in his presence. That's the only way we will win. In my "Yes" and in your "Yes," God breaks us down, then builds us back up. He is destroying bad habits, evil thoughts, acts of unkindness, unforgiveness, fear, and temptations. He builds us up to trust him, to depend on him for everything, and I mean everything. It's the same way God tested the children of Israel in the wilderness for 40 years to get them to trust him. He demonstrated how he provides for them by sending down manna from heaven to feed them daily and not allowing their clothes or shoes to wear out during that time, protecting them from the elements and the enemies. God wanted his children to depend on him and know that he would bring them out of every situation if they trusted him. Remember, for over 400 years, they were enslaved to the ways of the Egyptians, and that's who they were programmed to follow.

We are enslaved in the ways of this world and programmed to follow society, but God wants to change that in us. He wants us to shed the old habits of doing things that are sinful, he wants to change how we think, teach us how to represent him through our actions, and the things we say. I still am shocked at how easy "Christian men and women" can out curse the sinner man. The bible says that curses and blessings can't come out of the same mouth, James 3:10. We sometimes forget in moments that we belong to God, and that we are not to speak unkind words and curse someone to death. You can kill with your tongue; did you know that? How can we curse someone today and then pray for them tomorrow? Or even in our daily conversations. The tongue is a powerful tool. How it is used determines whether it brings good or harm. I often wonder about the purpose of using profanity when someone already has a strong point to make. Does profanity truly make the message clearer or have more impact? Or does it distract from the truth, especially for a child of God? You know, like when you are yelling at your kids and punctuating it with profanity. Or when you are telling a story or joke, does profanity make it come across better? I don't know, but it should be left on the tongues of the unsaved, and not the Christian.

Stop playing with God. I'm telling you, we reap consequences. We are God's chosen people; we are set apart. That means we live in this world, but we are not of the world. We shouldn't do what we see the world do. Yes, they will hate us, ridicule us, and lie about us for no reason, but know that your reward will be so great if you don't give in to the temptations that surround you. It's easy to fall into the pattern of the people you are around daily because you don't want to feel left out. We are not alone. Jesus said he will never leave you nor forsake you (Hebrews 13:5). We serve a true and living God. He is Holy, so when we come before him, we must show respect in our service. He is not one to be disrespected. That's what we do when we use profanity instead of blessings. Know the character of our God. He is not man, so be respectful and represent him correctly. He is connected to us. He pursues us and dwells in our temple. Don't think that he doesn't see what we do. Try not to become a stranger by placing distance between yourself and God. He won't dwell with you if you continue to sin, because life gets real and you need him by your side.

Chapter 6 - Surrendered Heart

If you have a heart for the Lord, you will want to surrender to his will because you know that he loves you and that he is all in for you. He wants the best for us, all the way to eternity. He doesn't want to contend with the world for our love. He is sad when we choose the things of this world over his love. Or when we choose material things, or other possessions over him. He is God, make no mistake, but I think we frustrate him. We tend to have selfish hearts, in all honesty, which is why he must cleanse and purge us and turn our thinking around. We tend to listen to the enemy of this world too much when we are not in the Word of God. Our thoughts get us in trouble; they lead us to act without seeking the Lord's guidance. Who do you choose to hear? You're going to listen to one or the other.

We can't hear God's voice when we're too busy focused on Facebook, Instagram, or TikTok. Nothing wrong with this until you are listening more to what they are saying than the voice of God. He says my sheep knows my voice. Are you his sheep? Remember, what the world has to offer is only temporary; the world itself is temporary. Salvation is eternal. Eternal is a long time to be without the Lord, I'm just saying. Look at how King David loved God, how he surrendered to him. Look how God blessed him. David was a shepherd boy when God anointed him to be King; he went through the process of becoming who God saw in him before he became King. What God has spoken to you will come to pass; I don't care how long it takes you to get in alignment with the Lord. His words do not return to him void; He doesn't lie. He knows our future, so he knows when you are ready for the promises. He knows when you are prepared to receive them, and they will be right on time.

Chapter 7 - Pride

Pride before a fall. "Pride goes before destruction, and a haughty spirit before a fall", Proverbs 16:18. Have you ever met someone who was so full of pride that you could not tell them anything? They must always be right about everything. They can't even ask for help because they see themselves as the only one who can figure it out, and asking would put them on the same level as you. Those are the type of people that God won't deal with. They won't surrender to the Lord; their heart posture is turned away from him. However, our merciful God will give them chances to humble themselves. 2 Chronicles 7:14 says, "if my people who are called by my name, will humble themselves and pray and seek my face and turn from their wicked ways, then will I hear from heaven, and I will forgive their sin and heal their land" now I know this scripture is talking about a nation, but remember we have nations full of prideful individuals who are turned away from God, and until we get back in his presence, we will continue to experience turbulence.

God will send us into the wilderness until we learn our lessons. He loves us, but just like any parent who wants their child to "act right," God will take his loving arms of protection from around us, which means the enemy can cause all kinds of mischief in our nation, in our communities, and in our lives. Until we decide to seek him, with hearts postured towards him in humble adoration. The beauty of being humble is that we open ourselves to allow God to lead us; we are not fighting him for control. We have surrendered hearts to the one who will take care of us (and know that when God takes care of us, he also uses people to do that, so don't miss your blessing by denying others help). Stubbornness is also not of God, and it's not cute. It's annoying, and if it's annoying to us down here, then it annoys God, you know why? Because it is not in his character, it shouldn't be in ours. We should always know who we are in Christ.

We understand our position with God: He is the supplier, and we are the recipients of all the goodness He has for us. The opposite of humility is pride, and according to 1 Peter 5:5, *"all of you be subject one to another, and be clothed with humility: for God resisted the proud and gives grace to the humble."* We must be very careful with how we see our place in God. I was one who listened when preachers said what was due us just for being a child of God, as if God owed us for living. The way I perceived it had me puffed up, prideful, and expectant. That can be dangerous. A heart full of pride can have us thinking that everything we have comes from us; we did the hard work, we saw what we wanted, we went after it, so it belongs to us. No credit to the Lord. God owns cattle on a thousand hills; he created us, we belong to him, yes, we do. If you are his, you will know it, want it, cherish it, and bask in it. Pride is not good in any shape, form, or fashion. It will put you on a pedestal too high for even God to reach, and God alone is the High and Lofty One that inhabits eternity. I'm not talking about being proud of an accomplishment or having pride about who you are. It would be a shame for you to think you were meeting God for eternal life, only for him to do to you what he did to Satan with all that pride, Revelation 12:7-12. That's right, kicked out of heaven and doomed to eternal death.

God is preparing us for his second coming, but he needs us to have a servant's heart and a humble spirit so that he can work on us and within us. Sometimes our lives take us down paths we would not normally take. Life's trials put us in certain situations, and we become overwhelmed, leading us to seek our own ways of coping with them. Trials come to give us strength, to encourage us, and to teach us, but in some cases, we can't handle the trials of life, so we may submit to things like substance abuse to make us temporarily forget our problems, to give false strength and bravery. Any abuse of anything used to hide what we are feeling on the inside is a lie (I know what you're thinking, but I did none of that, and I'm still not perfect; perfection will come with our glorified bodies, and we are no longer on this earth). Is it pride that keeps us from being authentic? Or maybe it is fear of exposing the true you and of no one liking that version. Are we too proud to truly apologize? Because it requires genuine humility to do that, to admit that we are at fault.

We destroy relationships with our actions or lack thereof, we can't pretend that we haven't offended someone or try to pretend it didn't happen by never speaking about it, we do a disservice to others when we try to cover up a wrong. A wrong does not bounce off the person who was wronged. Pretense is just faking it. We pretend to be okay when we know we are not. Pretending to be strong when we are weak, happy when we are sad. Healthy when we know we are sick. That's giving us false hope. My advice: seek help if you need it. Mental health is real. God wants us to be transparent, to walk in holiness. To be truly you in a good way. Not that person who's being "REAL" but doing everything wrong.

Do it God's way, it's more rewarding. Now I'm not saying it will be easy or instant, because it's a process, but we must be in the right heart posture to receive it.

Can you imagine living a lonely life because everyone thinks you are good? Pride hides transparency, pride hides hurt. What? I'm not hurt; life is good. Let's see, pride won't let you speak on infidelity in marriage, or an addiction, or abuse, physically or mentally, you're holding it in because you don't want everyone to know that things are broken. It's isolating. You miss out on good, Godly advice, compassion, and comfort. I'm not saying trust everyone, I'm not saying blast it to the world, but don't let pride keep you from healing so you don't become bitter or faithless. These are just a few examples.

Hurt has many faces; I am overcoming hurt by being transparent about my feelings and being vulnerable with the Lord, who has revealed many things I have been holding in. So, I am trying to share my feelings one step at a time, one person at a time. The right timing is important. Be careful, pride can cause pain. How? You hurt the people around you because they are trying to penetrate that wall of ego, stubborn, stoic, condescending, unmoving, selfish personality, and it can cause isolation, sour relationships, anger, and bitterness. Once we've encountered your pride for so long, we put our guard up, and sometimes it's hard to bring it back down. We try to distance ourselves from the person that you are. But a heartfelt apology, asking for forgiveness, can bring forth healing and reconciliation. Humility is key, and pray, always pray. God can heal all things, but you must believe that you are worthy of being healed, to believe in God's power to heal and not in your own. Nothing is too hard for God. Do you believe it?

Chapter 8 - My "Yes"

I say all of this because my "Yes" led to my journey of being transformed by God. I have truly grown up in Christ. Through my studies, I have learned a lot and gained a lot of experience. Nothing like a storm to put some gray hair on your head. Nothing like tribulations to humble you. It will make you think about the path you were headed in and will turn you around. I pray for his wisdom to help me make the right decisions. I don't get it right all the time, but I am trying every day. I try to let his presence overshadow me, so that you see him in me. No, I am still not perfect. I try to be a great mom, but I sometimes fail at that.

I remember when my baby girl was about 3 or 4 years old. We were at church and had to go to an evening service at a sister church. My children normally rode with my sister during those times. When it was time to go, we all got in our cars and left. At the other church, I asked my sister where my daughter was, and she said she didn't ride with her. At that moment, everything flooded back to my memory. My daughter fell asleep on the church bench, and with all the hustle and bustle, I walked out of the church without her. You can't imagine how panicked I was trying to get back to her.

My family called her at the church while my sister-in-law drove us back to pick her up. We walked into the church, and it was dark in there. All I could think was that my baby was left in a dark church alone, but also that God gave her a lifeline when my family called her on the phone; she heard and answered it. When I saw her, she was on the phone with them. I still feel the gripping fear sometimes when I think about that time and how imperfect I felt in that moment.

Or the time when we lived out of state and were at a barbecue with friends, my oldest girl almost drowned right in front of me. She was about 15 years old, and I was standing by the poolside because we didn't know how to swim, but there was a lifeguard there. My daughter was in the shallow end of the pool, and I remember telling her to be careful: "Okay," she said. I was talking to one of the guests when I turned my head for a moment. When I turned back around, I saw her head underwater, going deeper. I yelled to the lifeguard, "Get her!" he jumped in and grabbed her. I remember her saying that she was praying and asking God to forgive her for her sins because she thought she was about to die. I was in tears, and as I write this, I am crying.

As parents, we are responsible for our babies. We cover them in prayer if we pray. I'm so grateful for that covering. I don't care how much we prepare for things; nothing is foolproof. I had to realize that I am not perfect, but through God's saving grace, He gives us opportunities to do better.

In my book of poetry, I wrote many poems during the process of God purging me. One of the poems stood out, "The Complainer", which was me, complaining about circumstances. I had to shed that character flaw because it was not how God saw me. Complaining can turn into bitterness and negativity; it's acidic, eats through your soul, and spreads to others. To be honest, I didn't want to be this ungrateful person who believed that what I have isn't enough, or as if I don't appreciate the life I have. God revealed so many things in my life that needed changing. I didn't think they were issues, but God didn't like them, so they had to go. I love the person that I am becoming. Sometimes we get caught up in the different roles that we portray in life. We chase whatever makes us feel good about ourselves, temporary pleasures. Temporary happiness. The day I was born again, my God, it was the greatest feeling! And I still chase that feeling today. I sometimes think about what I was doing and try to reenact it. Being in the presence of God is like nothing else. He gives me joy, peace, happiness, safety, self-control, and so much more. There is nobody like our God. You must know that it still doesn't mean you won't go through some tough times in life; you will still stumble, but you will have him by your side.

Let me tell you, while I am chasing after God, I go through so many things that they're about to break me down. The mental assault is crazy. My journey takes me through so many levels; surrendering every day to the will of God is challenging, but I do it because he is worth it. My thoughts are sometimes not the thoughts of the Lord. (I often want to run from the process of becoming) I had to shed my way of thinking and try to figure out what God was trying to do, yes, I even have moments of why this is happening to me. I get very frustrated, angry, and sad; the emotions are highs and lows, but surrender was inevitable. I was tired of repeating the tests, but I wasn't giving up. The devil is a liar! Allowing God to guide me daily is what I learned to do. The process can be rough, but it is achievable; it has good days and bad days, and I work hard not to complain. Don't let anyone tell you that you must be strong all the time or that you can't have feelings about your struggles, and that nothing should bother you in your walk with God. If that were the case, God would not have put scriptures in the bible to encourage us to be strong and courageous. He knows what we are going through; the scriptures teach us how to lean on him for guidance.

God wants us, so he does what he does to get our attention. He wants to save us, be mindful that some challenges God will send into our lives; and for some, he will allow challenges to interrupt our lives, but in both cases, these are challenges that God uses to bring us to greater strength and maturity. Don't go through these challenges without the Lord. He is our peace, courage, and strength. Say yes to being transformed. The brand new you will appreciate the change.

Chapter 9 - Through God's Eyes

You don't need to be validated by anyone, even those who you think are for you. Your journey is your own, so don't allow others to dictate how God wants you to walk. Your relationship with God is between the two of you. If you trust him, he will guide you through your journey. Even through the rough places, or the lonely places, so listen to his voice, turn the TV off because it's hard to hear with all that chatter. It's only a distraction to get your mind off the Lord.

Now, I'm going to take you on a partial journey with me, to show you how God has been transforming my life from the old me to the new me. It's my journey to becoming who God sees in me, who he sees me to be throughout my life. Who better than the creator to see something good in us? Our God, who is perfect, looks down at the imperfect and sees us as more than the world condemned us to be. He knows our end from the beginning and loves us despite all our wrongs.

Fall in love with God. He is greater than anything your heart clings to on this earth. Rest in the arms of our Lord. He's got us. The times we feel alone in our struggles can be very daunting; it feels unreal, and you may ask yourself, “Is this really happening to me, and how can I get out of it?” Trust God. Give yourself time to think, because if you listen to yourself, you may do the wrong thing and go totally against what God wants to do in your life. His timing is perfect, and it is good.

Chapter 10 - His Plan

Life is a journey. It is full of many surprises, distractions, disappointments, and victories. We have choices in life, to go left or right. We try to follow a path we think will take us to higher heights. Some are successful, some are not. Some things last, some don't, which is why the journey of life should be followed by the one who created life. The bible said in Jeremiah 29:11, *"For I know the thoughts that I have for you", says the Lord. "They are plans for good and not for disaster, to give you a future and a hope".*

Jesus came that we might have an abundant life. He didn't say that we wouldn't go through some rough patches or that we wouldn't have to climb some difficult mountains. God's hand is in every part of our lives. But you know what? Our plans must align with his plans; we must pray for the will of God, and he will guide us along the way. You know how, when your parents are cheering you on, when you took those first steps as a toddler, after you kept falling? God was there; or learning how to ride your bike and run it into garbage cans or a ditch, and you picked it up and tried again? God was there. What about as an adult, when you were working towards a promotion, but someone was trying to block it, and you persevered and got it anyway? God was there. Each instance required you to press forward with determination, to follow the guidance of your parents or leadership to overcome obstacles.

How do you know that God is not guiding you through your journey both then and now? Often, we blame God when bad things happen, but why don't we think God is there when all the good things are going on in our lives? We don't give him credit for that but are quick to point out what he didn't stop or do for us, and not give ourselves any credit for our part in the situation. We even forget to say thank you when we know it could only be God, right? Why do we think that everything is cut and dry with God? Just like most companies implement processes to make things run smoothly, God also takes us through a process to help our lives run smoothly. The difference is that an employee will comply with a company's rules and adhere to mandated processes.

People tend to get mad at God for taking them through a process that will better their lives; some will turn their backs on him or leave the faith altogether. Don't get me wrong, it is not for the faint of heart. God does not play about salvation. You must be real with him. Remember, God knows the heart. You can't pretend with God. You can fool me, but not him. He is wisdom. But you won't know it if you don't get to know and trust him with your life.

While my husband and I lived in Memphis, we were in our first home. I remember the recession was happening, and we were struggling to make our monthly mortgage payment, which led to a financial crisis. I wasn't working at the time because I was in nursing school, and my husband was barely working. A friend mentioned a program called NACA that could help us with our mortgage payments. I told my husband about it, and at first, he didn't want to because he was embarrassed. But over time, he finally agreed. We had scheduled an appointment to determine our eligibility for assistance. When they took our information, they asked for our check stubs. I didn't have any, and my husband only had T-checks. We were told they couldn't accept the T-checks; they needed to be check stubs, which we didn't have. So, we left very disappointed, and we prayed for something to happen. A day later, we received a call from them saying they could accept the T-checks. Hallelujah! God will work it out! When they got all the information, they told us to call in every week, which we did. A year passed, and we did not have to make one mortgage payment; our battles were being fought. When the final decision was made, our mortgage payment was less than $1,000.00 per month. God is so good! We were going through some disappointing times; it was distracting, but full of surprises, because we couldn't believe how God was taking care of us. And then, to be victorious in keeping our home, the circumstances will be better than before. No balloon mortgage, no two mortgages, no high monthly mortgage. Y'all, it was worth the journey.

Chapter 11 - Walking By Faith

Your journey is your own. We don't share the same journey, because what God is doing in your life is different from mine, but what I do know is that every believer is expected to have faith in what God is doing in their own life. 2 Corinthians 5:7 says to *"walk by faith, not by sight"* Every person on this earth has an encounter with God in some way, an opportunity to be saved, because God is Merciful and Just, you won't get a chance to say that you didn't know, there are too many things in this world now that introduces you to the Lord, you have to listen and receive it.

Listen, one thing I have learned in my journey is that unexpected things can happen in my life, i.e., the death of my husband, car breaking down, the flooded basement, financial woes, all these things I saw happening to me, they were tangible, hurtful distractions that at first took my focus off the Lord. I was walking by sight, and that brought about anxiety, stress, hurt, pain, and fear. Y'all, it had a hold of me. There were times when I was on the floor bawling my eyes out. I was hurting so much that I couldn't breathe. I wanted to curl up in bed and wallow in my pain, but we can't do that for long because it gets so comfortable being in that misery that it can consume your life, and you will crave it. One day will turn into one year, and before you know it, it's an appendage that you can't get rid of. You are absorbed in it. You can't live without it; it will grow other appendages, like depression. You may become this negative person who can't see or won't see any good in people or situations. So don't get caught up. I had to learn constantly how to walk by faith. And for sure, it is scary, who wants to walk deliberately into the unknown? We are nosy by nature, right? We want to know every step that we take; I know I do. But that's not how God works; He wants to know that you trust him and have faith in him to lead you to where you need to go. Well, do you? Sometimes the walk that God has for us is to walk into new territory, new jobs, new city, new country, or new relationships. And y'all that journey may be on your own.

He wants to elevate us, make changes in our lives to equip us for the elevation, but he must strengthen us to fight the new devils that we will encounter. It's called surrendering to his will, not an easy task at all. Why? Because we can't let go of the reins called control, but once we do, it is freeing. No worries because we have released it to the Lord, unless we allow them back in. Psalm 46:10 says, *"Be still and know that I am God!"* I had to learn not to make moves centered on fear because of what was going on in my life. Fear will paralyze you from stepping into your purpose, and when you are afraid, you're telling God that you don't trust him. I learned how to trust God as my provider, my healer, my rescuer, my only source, even when I didn't see anything happening. It wasn't instant trust. I couldn't just say it with my lips. I had to let go, to surrender, and know that God will move. Not for the sake of myself, not for the sake of others, God moves at his appointed time. Period.

My trusting God in my 2006 Chevy Silverado every day, back and forth to work, was something I had to work on. Let me tell you, this truck has bled me financially. The breakdowns have been many. Frustrating for me, I have had so much anxiety when I drive it. Until one day, an epiphany occurred. God wants me to trust him with my truck, but more than that, because it's not about the truck but what it represents, the truck is just the vessel for me to trust God to take care of me. I tell God that I trust him, and he makes me prove it. I pray over that truck every time I enter it, from the hood to the engine, the tires, to the tailgate. I play sermons or encouraging podcasts all the way to work and back, focused on the Lord. Lately, I have just been opening my heart and talking to the Lord on the way to work. I don't feel anxious when I do this because the distractions of every bump or sound from the truck don't hold my attention. And before I knew it, I made it to my destination safely, and my trust in God has increased a little more every day.

Another testimony, I just recently had an encounter with the Holy Spirit. I was getting ready to leave my dad's home when I felt this quivering feeling in my stomach. It wouldn't go away. My brother walked me to my truck and watched me get in. I started my truck, and the ignition didn't catch, so it shut off. When I started it again, it caught, and I pulled off. I had to get gas, and I wanted to take the fastest route, which would have been the expressway, but the Holy Spirit put Torrence on my mind, so when I got close, I turned on Torrence, which was a street, and I took it all the way to the gas station near my home, because yes, it's cheaper. So, once I filled my tank up, Jiffy Lube came to mind, but I was tired and had a long day. I just wanted to go home, but the Holy Spirit had another agenda for me. I got in the lane for Jiffy Lube and pulled in. I asked the guy to check my oil, and he asked me to pop my hood. Once I popped the hood and he let it up, the latch fell off. I couldn't believe it because I had just recently gotten it fixed. I am telling you that at that moment, all I could think about was "what if I got on the expressway?" What if I didn't listen to the Holy Spirit's promptings? The guys at Jiffy Lube were able to get a rope and tie it down better than the latch did. I felt safe. I thanked my Lord for his covering.

He keeps his promises to protect me. No weapon formed against me shall prosper. My only source. (I know, and God knows that I need a new vehicle, don't get it twisted, God will provide. Just like he did for the children of Israel for 40 years in the wilderness.

Chapter 12 - God As My Defender

God as my Defender, this has been a long journey of him defending me against bullies and predators and protecting me from seen and unseen dangers. The Holy Spirit has been bringing back to memory even those instances when I was young, I remember a time when I was around middle school age, I was a patrol guard for my school, we had a crossing guard that I was on the same corner as she; one day I was walking to my corner, not paying attention to my surroundings because I have never had any issues with anyone bothering me, because I stayed to myself. Then one day someone grabbed my left shoulder and spun me around and hit me in the nose and was about to hit me again but I blocked it with all my strength, the guy had on a cap, he was taller than me and stout and around my age, his fist was almost at my face again when the crossing guard ran across the street yelling for him to get away from me and he ran. I was shaken up because I didn't know who he was. I didn't bother anyone to have enemies. The crossing guard asked me if I knew him, and I told her that I didn't, so she instructed me to watch out for him. I did that for a week, and when I didn't see him again, I relaxed. The minute I let my guard down, the enemy swarmed me, literally. I was on my way home from school, patrol was over, so I was going down the alleyway, and suddenly, I was surrounded by ten boys. They circled me, and one of them kicked me. The boy who hit me on the nose the week before was there as well, so I assumed that he was the one who got them together. They were just standing around me trying to figure out what to do, when they started talking, everyone couldn't hear so they moved closer to hear, when they did that, an opening was made down towards the back alley to my home, (look at God making a way) everything was racing through my mind at once, I thought, okay they are moving out of my way and I can get away now, but before I made my move, I was determined to kick that boy who kicked me, and that's what I did, I kicked him in the shin and shot down that alley, the brother to the boy who started it all came chasing after me (I found out later that they were brothers, twins). I guess he thought he was fast because he had long legs, but I wasn't slowing down, (I was like Elijah outrunning King Ahab's chariot in the bible lol) y'all I felt my victory when I got to the row of houses and I started yelling, "MOMMA!" he did one last ditch to grab at me but I sped up and was in the vicinity of my home, I saw that he had stopped at the row of houses, but I kept going till I was home safe. Now ask me if I let my guard down again.

I'll use this as an analogy for how we are caught off guard by the enemy because we are not alert to the fact that he is always lurking, watching, and ready to attack. We get comfortable, and we are not strong enough to fight the enemy. If we are not walking in the spirit, we can't handle him. But God had my back because my mom was walking in the spirit, and her prayers were covering me. Thank the good Lord!

Satan goes after our youth; he wants to destroy our innocence. That's why we need to pray for each other. Some people don't have a parent's prayer to cover them, but if you can, if you want the best for others, pray for them with a sincere heart. Because if you pray with malice, you'd better dig two ditches. Your fall will come soon after. So be nice. Another testimony of God's protection, I remember one night when my parents were at my aunt's house, one of my older male cousins came by our home unannounced, my sister's and I shared a room and we were in there when one of my younger brothers let him in, he came up to our room and stood in the doorway, while we sat on our bed, he was talking in a soft tone, teasing us, I guess to get us to relax, but we did not trust him and we did not move at all. When he saw that we were not falling for his deceit, he left. Another failed attempt by the enemy. My sisters and I discussed it after he left. I felt uncomfortable; I didn't like the way he was looking at us, and I especially didn't like the fact that he knew my parents were with my aunt, which is where he usually was; he didn't let them know that he was coming over because my parents wouldn't have allowed it. I told my mom about it. I don't know what happened, but he never attempted that again, nor was he around us. People are heartless and selfish; they don't care that what they do to the young will shape how they move through life, how it can break them, how it can shape them into disturbed individuals, how they sometimes grow to hurt others, and it becomes a generational cycle.

Prayer is so important for the protection of this world. It's how we reach God and develop an intimate relationship with him so that we can learn how to develop those good characteristics of our Father. A loving Heavenly Father produces a loving child if we follow him. It's also how we petition his throne. He said the righteous run into his strong tower and are safe (Proverbs 18:10). We must get back to prayer. Prayers can help us if we do them, and if we don't do them, it can hurt us because again, the enemy is always lurking and waiting to destroy us. Prayers have helped my past, present, and for my future. All I know is that I am safe in his arms, no other place I'd rather be.

Chapter 13 - God Orders Our Steps

God orders our steps. If your journey leads you to buying a house, or a car, or choosing a school, job, or career, don't leave God out of your decision-making process. Matthew 6:33 says *to "seek ye first the kingdom of God, and his righteousness and all these things shall be added unto thee"*. Y'all, it's a faith walk, it is believing and not seeing, it is waiting and standing. Just because we want it right now doesn't mean we can handle it right now. We get so upset with God because he has not delivered his promises when we want them. Some leave the faith because they don't want to wait or have stopped believing it was going to happen. In due time, in due season, when he knows you can handle it, when you start to seek him first and not just want what he can give you.

Don't try to use God, because he knows and he feels too. I'm here to tell you that he will deliver. Just believe. Before my late husband and I bought our home, we prayed for it for two years, and while we were praying, we worked on getting our credit together. My late husband had something on his credit report that needed to be corrected. We kept checking his credit report, it was still there. One day,

I heard a whisper, "check his credit," and an urging to look at his credit report, because we had stopped looking for a while. So I checked his credit report and didn't see the derogatory mark on it. I called my husband and shared what I saw in the report, and he said, "Call the bank! Let's get this going." When we called the bank, they reviewed our report, and everything was as we said. We were able to move forward with purchasing a house. Our home had everything we were praying for. God proves that if we seek him, things will fall into place. Now let me tell you, sometimes it will be a wait. God does not get in a hurry. It is a process, remember?

What God wants is for us to be good stewards of the things that he blesses us with. Some things we can handle better when we are stronger, mind, body, and spirit. That's why God purges us; He takes us through some things to discipline us and to remove the impure elements in our lives. He gives us strength to overcome it, making us stronger for the new levels we are entering, so that the enemy can't weaken our defenses and make us lose what we have been given. The purging is tough but remember this: if it didn't take you out, you will be stronger for it. I mentioned my late husband's old truck earlier; I am riding around in it. I think it's about ready to go to the car grave. God's thoughts are not mine lol, because he is sustaining that truck.

Remember…children of Israel, wilderness, 40 years? Yeah, that part. God has shown me and promised me a new truck, but he has not yet made a way for me to get it. I know it's coming, and I am being obedient and waiting, because he told me to stand. It's a part of the process; he is instilling patience in me. I have been teased, talked about, told to stop being cheap, asked to sell my parts for their truck, etc. Yes, I feel some way about it. I did cry out to the Lord about it, and then went in search of a vehicle, any vehicle, because of the fear and embarrassment I let enter. But then, I remembered God's promise, and I prayed over the truck I have. And you know, I drive on the expressway daily and see brand new cars that are stopped on the side of the road, and I keep driving to my destination. He's keeping my truck together until I have learned what he wants me to know. Matthew 7:7-8 says, *"ask and ye shall receive, seek and ye shall find, knock and the door shall be opened unto you."* God's timing is perfect, but we must be ready for it.

Chapter 14 - Don't Journey Alone

Our journey does not have to be alone; if we choose to let him walk with us, he will. Yes, I'm talking about our Lord. I know, the things that happen in the dark, you don't want to come to light. But because Jesus is light, he will uncover all that is done in the dark. That might be the problem for some, right? It feels good to do the things we want to do without thinking of the consequences or thinking that God is not watching us. That's how the enemy fools us; he makes us think that we are invisible, that we can hide our sin. That the decisions we make in life can go unchecked.

Our destiny is our own; that is true. But be careful. If we decide to walk after this world, to lust after this world, to ignore the words of the Lord that are everywhere for us to see and hear, know that what happens at the end of our life is the decision of our Lord, and at that point, your destiny is in his hands. Matthew 16:26 says, "*For what is a man profited, if he shall gain the whole world, and lose his own soul? Or what shall a man give in exchange for his soul?*" Meaning the soul has eternal value, and we take the chance of losing it for temporary worldly gains. I don't care if we gained all that the world can offer. Chasing after the world instead of chasing after Christ will lead to eternal death. Is it worth it? Our life span may be up to 100 years, and that's not long compared to eternity.

Listen, if you belong to the Lord, obedience to his will and his ways is going to be something that you will want to do. Believe me, the difference between someone who is a born-again believer and someone who uses the title of "Christian" is very different. I'm not talking about the watered-down Christianity that allows you to do and say whatever and then hide behind the title. No judgment, God is the only one who will judge, that's for sure. I'm just saying, if you grew up in church but are no longer walking with the Lord, and by that, I mean you have not taken up your cross to follow him, submitted to his will, stopped intentionally sinning, you may want to ask yourself whether you are truly born again. That was me, so this is not judgment, but how can you know the voice of God if you don't know him? How will you know he is ordering your steps? "*Study to show thyself approved unto God, a workman that need not to be ashamed, rightly dividing the word of truth*", 2 Timothy 2:15.

I used to be that Christian who relied on the pastor to read the scriptures, break them down in a sermon on Sundays, and that was all the food I ate for a week. Honestly, I didn't know that I needed to go deeper in my relationship with the Lord, because I thought I was good. He got my attention. When God gets your attention, it's usually in a big way so that we can seek him out. Trials and tribulations will do that. Now I seek him daily, so I am prepared for the enemy's attack. I know who God is, my strong tower. In his words, I can't be fooled by the enemy. I know what God will do for me. He is never-ending. I will always continue to learn from him. He is our weapon against Satan.

Chapter 15 - A Different Kind of Love

The journey of love, first, I want everyone to know that Jesus loves you, and that nothing can separate you from his love. I don't care where you go, how low, or what you do; Jesus loves us, but don't take him for granted. John 14:15 says, "*If you love me, you will keep my commandments*". Yeah, that one was hard. To keep God's commandments meant shedding things that life teaches you to hang on to, those things society deems 'it's okay'.

Let me tell you, I had to let go of some things, i.e., unforgiveness, complaining, anger, disregard, selfishness, etc., not to mention the thought processes, the acceptance of things in our lives that God says no to, when we allow what we watch on TV to penetrate how we view life as the world views it. As Christians, a lot of what we see should lead us to prayer. We should not have love for the world, but only for the things of God, who is our leader. We must pray for this world and love the people, but hate sin, including our enemies. Even to the point of loving at a distance. God was building my character to look like his. What is it you ask? Godliness. Living the life God wants me to live. To demonstrate his characteristics of love, joy, peace, kindness, etc. My love journey is lifelong, but I truly became aware of the journey when things started falling apart in my life, and I had only him to depend on; he showed me who he was for me, and I will always love him for taking care of me. You never forget the one who rescued you. God said he would never leave me; he stuck with me through it all. Yes, there were times when I thought he did leave me because life was hard, but he carried me through it.

When my husband got sick and died, it was a trickle-down effect. I had financial problems, house problems, problems with my children, with my truck, with family relationships, with my job, and people were cheating me out of money, and I couldn't do anything. My life was chaos. I was in battles with my mortgage company that left me feeling defeated; I didn't feel supported. I felt so helpless and alone. That's what the enemy wants: to get you alone when you are down and pounce on you. He will put thoughts in your head against those who love you. I had begun to get bitter towards my family, my friends, because I was drowning and no one was saving me. Or so I thought. God was sending help, but I was going through so much, one thing after the other, that it didn't seem as if anyone was there with me. I had tunnel vision lol. What I had to realize was that the feelings of being let down were not because others didn't care, but because they were unable to let go of the awkwardness around my circumstances.

At first, I couldn't understand what was happening; it overwhelmed me like a tornado for several months to a couple of years. I didn't know if I was coming or going. I was praying to God superficially because, as I said before, at that time, I thought I was good in my relationship with him. He wasn't answering. I couldn't sleep, so I woke up between 1, 2, and 3 a.m. because of stress, then got up at 5:30 a.m. for work, only to deal with that drama on top of everything else. No one saw the turmoil that was raging within; they didn't care, and so I mentally checked out at work, too. (I want to note that just because people don't wear their sorrows for all to see, it doesn't mean they are okay. Check on them, especially if something tragic has happened in their life. It is not okay to be desensitized to others' feelings. God gave us empathy; we should use it.) I was trying to get control in some way. I had to rethink how I was moving. What was I doing wrong? I used those early-morning wakeups to talk to God, and that was when I was led to read the scriptures. I really didn't know what to read, and someone mentioned a bible app, so I downloaded it, and the daily devotionals started coming to my phone.

So, every day I would wake up and read, but I wasn't understanding, so I downloaded Bible commentaries to know what I was reading and get a better understanding. I understood that God was preparing me for greater; he knew that I needed a character change, I needed strengthening, and he had to preserve me. I learned to truly praise God, so I started adding praise in the mornings, along with intentional prayers. Then, something happened, I had a vision so clear and seemed so real, but I didn't understand it, and I am still waiting for the Holy Spirit to reveal it. That was the first of many.

At that time, I heard an online pastor discussing dreams and visions from God that we sometimes mistake for déjà vu. It piqued my interest, and I started listening to her for guidance as my dreams were coming daily. I learned that it's one of the ways God speaks to us. God was teaching me through scripture, my dreams, and prayer; obedience, love, trust, faith, patience, and consistency, and was still teaching me how to wait well. I am in the orbit of the Lord. He has found me and keeps me safe; he tells me that he "sees me" that he “loves me”, that he is watching over me, my protector, he knows what I am going through and has been my comforter, my friend, my confidante. When I had no one else, God never left me. As he spoke to me, he was guiding me towards perfection and holiness. Of course, I’m still learning. I don’t think we will get there until we get to heaven. But we must strive for that perfection because our God wants us to be perfect and holy because he is. I didn’t realize that God was changing me; He was making me stronger and giving me courage. Teaching me how to walk right. I learned that I have power in the name of Jesus, and that he has given me and you the authority to rebuke the enemy from the attacks on our lives.

I was awakened at night by scary visions in my room and bad dreams; the enemy was trying to scare me from getting stronger in the Lord. I don’t know why the enemy thinks that scaring me will make me run from the Lord; it only made me draw nearer to the Lord for his protection. But I think that the enemy does scare others from getting closer to the Lord, saying “yes” will open your eyes to spiritual things, and that can be scary for some. It’s surprising, yes, but now that I have told you what to expect, don’t be afraid. Under God’s covering, the enemy can’t touch you.

When I found that out, I became more secure in my knowledge that I can ask God to keep me safe, and he will. I learned to ask God to guard my thoughts from the enemy, and he did. I now sleep without those bad dreams.

As time went on, I remember thinking, I just need to get through this difficult time and then all would be well. I was in bible class one Wednesday, and the question came up about the different levels in our journey, that as God takes you higher, you will encounter the enemy anew. I thought, "What?" It doesn't end? I got so frustrated that I wanted to quit. Well, guess what? You can't give up; you can't go back. My spiritual eyes were opened. If I quit, the enemy would have his way with me. But I must surrender to God? I was thinking that's like enslavement, God doesn't do that. Give everything up and depend on God. What? I couldn't believe it; I really had a difficult time with that (y'all, this was me at the beginning of my journey to learn and become). I remember getting angry because I was thinking, God wants me to be a slave? That is what it is basically. I questioned how it could be free will. But here's the deal. Who do you want to be a slave to? God or Satan? I never want to be a slave to Satan, so when we are serving God, that is liberty. God chose me, and I choose him right back.

I had to learn how to submit to God. I know that he loves me and wants the best for me. Submitting to God is an everyday practice I must cultivate in this journey. I choose every day to be obedient to God. To do the right thing, to think the right thoughts, and ask for forgiveness when I don't. Some days, it gets by me. Again, I'm not perfect, but I'm striving to be. I get an urge to take things into my own hands; my mind keeps trying to figure something out. Then I remember that I am trusting God to take care of me. I know that God cherishes me, and I want him to trust me with his love. I show him by learning what he requires of me. Study his word, live life that represents him. And I fasted. Fasting was something I didn't know how to do well. I had to do some research, and y'all when I tell you that God loves the sacrifice, I took it seriously. God responds; he communicates, usually through my dreams. It's amazing. He called me by my name, and my heart was overwhelmed.

My heavenly dad sees me. I'm not trying to make God look bad. I want him to look at me proudly. I am his daughter, and I want his light to shine within me so that he gets the glory. "Well done" is what I want to hear. Y'all, it's not easy all the time, but it is so rewarding. What he is birthing within me will have longevity, and it will not wither.

I wouldn't change anything about my process. My goal is heaven-bound, and I plan to do the work of the Lord to bring more souls to Christ. When you love someone, you work hard to make the relationship work. So, I try to walk in obedience to him. Don't get me wrong. I still mess up, but the Holy Spirit convicts me, and I ask for forgiveness or repentance. I'm not intentionally doing wrong, but it's still wrong.

I love God, so I don't want to disappoint him. I don't want him to wish he had never created me. I want to make him smile. When I know I resisted Satan and didn't fall into his trap, I look up towards heaven and say, "Are you proud of me?" When we are obedient, we show God that we love him. I don't know when or how God will manifest his promises; I just know that he will keep his word. The wait is long, but I know that had he given me his promises before my transformation, I would not have cherished it; I would have been unprepared for it and probably lost it. I trust him to guide me through this life. It's like with our earthly parents, we love them, we don't want to displease them, so we try to be obedient to them, and they reward us with their love. Our Heavenly Father loves us so much more, so we should be that much more obedient and grateful.

Chapter 16 - Are You Impatient?

A journey can be long and tedious, and we live in a time where people want everything right now, whether it is money, relationships, careers, or things. We don't like delays. Our eyes get as big as saucers when we look at what our neighbors have, and we want it, right now, no matter the cost. What happened to the saying, "good things come to those who wait," a quote attributed to British author Violet Fane (1892). People are too impatient to wait nowadays, so instead of good things coming your way, we have grown accustomed to having temporary things that give you a fleeting moment of satisfaction. And then you are looking for the next fix.

Psalm 37:7 says, "*Be still before the Lord and wait patiently for him; fret not yourself over the one who prospers in his way, over the man who carries out evil devices.*" Wait on the Lord to bless you with things that will be good and will last. Don't be jealous or envious of what your neighbor has; it doesn't do you any good to want it, get it, and be miserable with it because you didn't get it the right way. I would tell you to wait on the Lord. His strategy is much better. We have no idea what good things God has in store for us when we follow him. Rags to riches, pauper to prince, peace and joy that is overwhelming. These types of things, doing impossible things, unimaginable things, are what the Lord can do for those who follow him and wait.

1 Corinthians 2:9 says, "*no eye has seen, no ear has heard, and no mind has imagined what God has prepared for those who love him*". We shouldn't bypass the process; it's meant to prepare us for our future. The process equips us to maintain those blessings so that we become good stewards of what the Lord has gifted us. We can be unprepared for big blessings if we get them too soon. We can mishandle it, not appreciate it, or not be mentally prepared for its greatness. God absolutely knows what he is doing. He is for us. Do you trust him?

Chapter 17 - Crossroads

Your journey will lead you to a crossroad where you must choose your direction and the person you will become. It takes courage to walk a path that is not familiar or the norm deemed by society, to move forward while others fall behind, and to accept the loneliness that will come with it; because the loneliness is an important part of your journey, it's your walk with God so that you hear only him talking to you, transforming you, so don't be afraid of the loneliness, and also to realize that not everyone is meant to go with you.

Your journey is your own. It's scary, yes, but this is your time to truly trust in God to lead you to where he is taking you. Take my word for it, it's not easy being set apart. People are not kind when you go against what everyone else is doing. When you choose not to follow them, they reveal who they truly are. Don't let them into your headspace, no matter how kind or patient you try to be. Some people are uncomfortable with the light within you. They don't want prayer, compassion, or truth; they reject it. That isn't your fault. You can't change them; only God can. Be prepared, because they may laugh at you, spread gossip, lie about you, and do whatever they can to discredit your name. Stay rooted anyway.

Matthews 5:11-12 says, "*Blessed are ye, when men shall revile you, and persecute you, and shall say all manner of evil against you falsely, for my sake. Rejoice and be exceeding glad: for great is your reward in heaven: for so persecuted they the prophets which were before you.*" God chose you; he picked you; people are going to come for you regardless of what you do or say. Whether you are poor or rich, the light that God shines within you will be hated. They are coming for you, anyway, don't dim your light because of opposition. And let me say this, when God chose you, he intends to lead you, his way; he doesn't want anyone else taking his credit for your rise. Let them talk, let them naysay, let them wallow in their envy. What I'm saying is, don't let persecution stop you from going down the righteous road.

You heard the Lord, great is your reward in heaven and on earth. That's our destiny, our goal, right? We only have one life, one soul. Live life the way God intended, and he will give you the courage to continue your journey, no matter who or what comes against you. Continuing in the wrong direction will make us unsafe; we won't have any covering. The enemy (Satan, devil, etc.) will have access to us. Don't be fooled. He only wants to kill, steal, and destroy our lives, according to John 10:10. Believe it! Do you honestly believe that the enemy cares about you? He will use anyone or anything to knock you down. Which is why we need to stay in God's word, so that we know how to fight the enemy. God is our champion, our hero; he will fight our battles for us because we are his. You know how Dorothy from The Wizard of Oz had to follow the yellow brick road to get to the "Emerald City" to go home? Well, Christians must stay on the straight and narrow path to go home to our Heavenly Father. My advice… get on, stay on, and don't get off.

Purpose

Focused. The burden I carry,
Is the burden I will serve
It is what I was called to do
It is my purpose
I choose obedience over sacrifice
Purpose takes boldness
It is not for the weak-hearted
Sometimes the easy road seems clearer
That's not where my feet are aligned
God put me back on track
Because my purpose makes the impact
He tests me to see where my heart lies
He watches me to see what I will do
He requires my complete surrender
Because he knows that I must operate within my purpose,
The thing that he has called me to.
Focused. The trust from God over this purpose, this plan.
In my excitement, I received the message, and I ran.
To be a good steward over his charge
Whether big or small
I listened for my call
And move forward in my purpose

Chapter 18 - The Choices We Make

Your journey may lead you to people who may cause you to doubt who you are in Christ and question the path God has prepared for you. Don't allow their voices to stop you from moving forward in the direction God is calling you to. Deuteronomy 31:8 says, "*Do not be afraid or discouraged, for the Lord will personally go ahead of you.*" You must remember, they can't hear what God is saying to you, so they don't understand when you "stand" because God told you to. They want you to move when God never told you to go. They urge you to go when God clearly said to stay. They expect you to remain in the background, because that's where you have always been in their eyes. But they don't understand that God is now bringing you into the light. They want your silence, while God is calling you to be bold. They are comfortable with who you were, but God is revealing who you are becoming.

What they resist is not you, it's the change God is producing in you. When you follow God, his directions won't always be clear; you may question some of the things you see and hear and be tempted to be swayed from the path. You must stay in the Word of God for strength and courage.

Be obedient no matter what, it can be scary, the unknown, the new territory, but faith over fear. When I'm scared to do something, I pray and ask God for courage to complete the task. I would get in my head, thinking I would fail, or that someone would question what I am doing or why I am doing it, often making me doubt myself. The key is to push through, block out the looks and what they are or aren't saying, follow the plan, and don't ever give up.

The enemy doesn't want you to succeed, so often he will work through someone close to you, someone whose opinion you value, to plant a seed of doubt. Do not fall for it. Do not allow yourself to be pressured into applying for a job that is not for you or buying a new car simply because it is expected, but because God told you to do it. Let every other voice fade away. Their thoughts and their opinions should not dictate how you move in Christ. Obedience to God matters more than the approval of people. Simply put, you may have people close to you who try to give you good advice to follow, but it is wrong because that's not what God said to do. Also, you must understand that people have a natural inclination to be envious and jealous of what others are doing and try to sabotage it. People don't want to be left behind when they see you are growing; don't get caught in the web of the unfulfilled journey of others. This is the time you must remember what God said to you and follow the plan. Stay focused.

Chapter 19 - It's Not Easy

Nobody said the journey would be easy. You will run into much-needed adjustments. What I mean is that there will be lessons to learn, shedding ungodly habits, forgiving others when you don't want to, and praying for them. That's a big one, but it must be done. God has lots of people that he has called and chosen. Some of them are living the life of this world. They have not yet met the Lord. So, it is up to us to pray for them. We also must forgive. How long have you been holding a grudge against someone? Has it been five, ten, fifteen, or twenty years since you have spoken, holding on to anger, hatred, or unforgiveness? That would be insane. Over what? Can you even remember?

Matthew 6:14-15 says, *"For if you forgive men their trespasses, your heavenly Father will also forgive you. But if you forgive not men their trespasses, neither will your Father forgive your trespasses"*. So basically, if I forgive others for the things that have been done to me, our Heavenly Father forgives me for the things that I have done to him. I think that's fair. I am not trying to downplay anyone's tragedy. There are so many people who have been really wronged, hurt, and betrayed; the pain is indescribable. But do you know that God can heal you from that pain? He can help you forgive and be stronger for it, so you can overcome the destruction someone caused in your life. To be able to pray for them. To release you from that bondage, that stronghold the enemy has over your life, because you have decided to trust God and let go of the pain, disappointment, and anger.

2 Corinthians 10:4-5 says, *"For the weapons of our warfare are not carnal, but mighty through God to the pulling down of strongholds; casting down imaginations, and every high thing that exalts itself against the knowledge of God, and bringing into captivity every thought to the obedience of Christ."* We are in a spiritual warfare with spiritual enemies. When we come into the knowledge of Christ, our eyes are opened to the battle that has been moving in the world and in our lives since birth and before time. What some have experienced began in the spirit and manifested in the physical. The enemy wants to destroy our mind, body and spirit and any connection that we may have with God. Overcoming what has happened is important for growth. Who said it would be easy? I won't diminish anything that anyone has gone through, it's your truth but don't shrink back. No one is exempt from hurt in any shape, form, or fashion, but not everyone wants to forgive; to

forgive is to be free. They won't have a hold over your life anymore. When Jesus shed his blood on that cross, his blood freed us from so many things, but we must receive the gift. We must know how to take advantage of the benefits that he gave us through his blood. Follow the path that he leads you on. Just like he led me to develop a closer relationship with him, he will do the same for you. I had to learn how to forgive, not give up, not dismiss a wrong that was done, but to forgive them, and guess what else? Be able to sincerely pray for them and move forward in my life. Those whom the Lord set free are free indeed, John 8:36.

Chapter 20 - The Unknown

The journey of not knowing was a difficult one for me. I'm the person who needs to know the next steps so that I can be prepared. I don't want to wait for surprises. I am not a procrastinator. If I have a task to do, I like to get it done right away, as it frees up time for me to do other things and keeps me from feeling pressured. So, imagine my surprise when the Lord visited me in my dreams and told me things I had no clue what to do with. To this day, I'm still in the dark about some of the dreams God has been revealing little by little. Does it get frustrating? Yes. The Lord reveals when he knows I am ready for the revelation. Jesus is a great teacher. He taught us humility and patience. Humility and patience are big ones for me, but I think I am finally getting it. The funny thing is that he also taught me to trust him. Trust him in the unknown, when I do, he knows that I have surrendered another aspect of my life to him. For him to guide me in my journey.

The devil had another plan, though; he was throwing those fiery darts with an aim that was so precise, Robin Hood didn't have anything on him. He knew exactly where to hit to make it hurt, because he watched me and he watched you.

What does that mean? It means the problems I was facing, such as debt and my truck, etc. The enemy was targeting those things that were the center of my life. He knows my truck got me to work and back; he knows I don't like owing any debt. The enemy knows what is important to us, and if we are following Jesus, he is coming after us, after the things that are important to us. Remember, they are distractions to take our focus from Christ. Satan's tactics are the same, but if you lose focus, it will hit differently every time. Do not fear, fight back. I'm not telling you this to make you afraid. That is not of God. I'm telling you to be strong and courageous as our Lord has commanded us to do.

This is not the time to try to be safe so that the enemy will leave you alone. Trust me when I say that not knowing where God is leading you can be scary. Your understanding of your purpose is not clear, but the enemy knows something is happening in the spirit realm, and if your spiritual eyes and ears are open to the Lord, you know something is shifting. Pray consistently. God leads, and we follow. Not every step we take will be seen. When the fog comes to block our vision, remember we walk by faith, not by sight, but we must keep walking because we have work to do in the Kingdom of God. If God can't use you, he will use someone else. Don't get left behind because of fear of the unknown. We must know the difference between God testing us and the enemy attacking us.

God wants to transform us; the enemy wants to destroy us. I can tell that I am going through tests, because the storms that I am going through are not destroying me. All around me is chaos, but I am still standing. I am safe in the arms of my Lord. I don't know God's appointed time when he will manifest his promises. We can't become anxious when things don't happen at the time we expect them to, but we must remain expectant because it's coming. God doesn't lie.

This is your time to pray while waiting. I have experienced this more than once. In moments when I did not know if God would come through for me, I worried that help would not arrive in time, or even if it was meant for me. But he was there when I needed him. Not in the way I expected or wanted, but in the way that sustained me. He never failed me. Yes, I panicked at first because of the pressure of deadlines, but I had to remember who God is and what he promised he would do. He said, *"Seek ye first the kingdom of God and his righteousness, and all these things will be added unto thee"* Matthew 6:33. God is our source.

When we have bills to pay, car debt, or any other need, we must trust him to do exactly what he said he would do. If I follow his plan, seek him first, love him, and depend on him, he will provide what I need. So I go back to the beginning, back to his word. Life is a learning process, and thank God I am learning quickly. I was fasting intensely, truly seeking God. People wondered what was going on with me, but I was searching for him and asking for confirmation. Sometimes he gave it, and sometimes he did not. I had to wait for my answers. I had to wait for God to move. Yet even in the waiting, I knew he was already present and working everything out for me. The bible is our road map; he will guide us if we follow. God is funny sometimes; he won't answer your questions first, so you can believe he will. Nope, you must trust him, believe, and then receive. Trust the process.

Chapter 21 - Praise Your Way Through

Journey of praise. Praising God is what we were created to do. So why is it so hard to do it? I will say for me, it was hard because of the attacks that were going on in my life. I couldn't see the sun for all the rain clouds, my family was being attacked, my car was breaking down constantly, I was having difficulty with my mortgage company, my finances were acting funny, and I took my focus off God to focus on the problem. That was a no-no. Y'all I spiraled, I couldn't breathe, it was so painful, I was frustrated, and I was so tired, tired of everything happening to me with what seemed like no break. Someone suggested that I praise God, even in the middle of everything I was going through. But I didn't have the strength to do it. The words would not even form on my lips. They felt swollen from the spiritual beatings, still tender from the blows of life.

When I finally opened my mouth to praise, angry tears flowed, my heart started palpitating, and all I could think was, " Why so much? It was too much for me, honestly. The weight was heavy. Waiting for change day by day is hard. I hold onto hope, anticipating the manifestation, but when it does not come, I feel the ache of disappointment settle in. I try to guard my thoughts and emotions, so I do not spiral, because Satan waits for moments of doubt. That is where praise comes in. Praise is a sacrifice. It is a sound that breaks through the lies the enemy whispers. I thought about the song, "Praise is what I do." Even when we are going through difficult times, we should still praise God, because He is still worthy. He still sits on the throne. He is still for us.

"Come to me, all you who are burdened, and I will give you rest" (Matthew 11:28). I had to learn to give my burdens to the Lord, and when I finally did, I found peace through praising him. Praise helped me release the walls of hurt and anger, frustration, and hopelessness that had built up inside me. When I praise him, my focus returned to where it belonged, on God, loving him, and worshiping him. My troubles had been distancing me from God, but praise helped bring us back together.

I am no longer easily deceived by the enemy. I can recognize his attacks more quickly now because I once fell into those traps. I have truly learned so much. I am not saying that I know everything, but I have learned to use the power of praise whenever I see trouble coming my way. "Let everything that has breath praise the Lord", Psalm 150:6. It works, y'all, praise will get rid of those demons. Praise your way through all your woes. I trust God, and when I am in his presence, I can't hear the negative thoughts that the enemy tries to put in my mind. When I am worshiping and praising, my mind is focused on loving our Lord, and he rewards me by doing what I ask of him. Some immediately, now I'm talking about the little blessings that he does for me daily; like when I am navigating through traffic and I ask him to give me an opening in traffic, he does it, it's so amazing y'all because it's unexpected, but the way it happens lets me know that it was God, or when I ask for the rain to fall after I get to my destination and as soon as I get there, it rains. Or when I asked the Lord to make a way for my son to come home for Thanksgiving break because plane tickets were so high and I couldn't afford to buy the ticket, He did that within the week. I checked the airline and saw that they had a great sale, a round-trip ticket for $200, taxes included.

We must thank him for the small things, too. Some blessings are delayed. I'm still waiting for that big blessing to manifest, but we must stand strong in our wait, trusting and believing that it will come to pass. God loves us, and we should want to let him know that we love and appreciate him for who he is and for all that he does for us daily. Don't get me wrong, I'm not saying that you should walk around acting like a "holy roller," offering phony praises and pretending everything is fine. God knows your heart, and he knows whether it truly belongs to him. He sees sincerity, and honestly, I don't know why people try to pretend. You don't have to convince me or anyone else, because the only one who matters is God. Empty praise won't even make it past the church bench you're sitting on, let alone reach God. The truth is that praise isn't for God's benefit; it's for ours. We enter his presence with praise and thanksgiving, and he responds by pouring out his blessings. God already knows how great He is.

If we don't praise him, the rocks will cry out. Our praises help us. Praise is part of an intimate relationship with our Lord. Phony praise doesn't honor him; it only reveals what's really in our hearts. You may feel like God hasn't done anything for you, but pretending to praise him for the sake of others doesn't fool him. He knows when praise is empty, and that kind of praise is wasted. Instead, we could use that time to truly get to know who our Lord is and to understand what he will do for those who trust him. As we grow in our knowing him, he helps us trust that he will keep his word. That trust gives us security, even when we can't yet see the outcome.

We praise him not just for what we see, but because God is faithful and trustworthy. Every day is an opportunity for you to praise God. He is worthy of being praised. Really, when he sacrificed his life for our sins, was buried in the grave, and conquered sin, death, and Satan, and rose on the third day with all power in his hands, that was enough. Our praises should be with our whole heart, mind, and spirit, reaching the heavens and giving off a sweet-smelling perfume that pleases our Lord. Praise God. Honor him. He alone is worthy.

Chapter 22 - Trusting God's Promises

Trusting God's promises and obeying his word are not separate; you can't do one without the other. How can we say we trust him, but don't trust him enough to obey him when he tells us to do something? He keeps his promises if we obey his commandments. In other words, we receive blessings if we fulfill his will. Note that if you are a Christian, obedience is a very important part of your life. We trust God to move in our lives. God is going to test your trust in him; he will see if you are going to obey what he has told you, whether in a dream, a whisper, or a vision. Even when it looks strange, even when no one believes you, even when you are the odd man out. Trust what God has promised, know that it will happen, and it will manifest. Just keep the faith and don't give up, no matter how long it has been.

Even when it doesn't appear to be what you thought it would look like. I know that it is easier said than done, when you don't see it, you lose faith. You begin to doubt, or you get tired of believing that God will come through. Your excitement has started to wane. We *"walk by faith, not by sight",* 2 Corinthians 5:7. God doesn't have to prove anything to us. He is sovereign; he does what he wants, when he wants. He's our creator, not the other way around. As a parent, I know my children; each one has their own way of thinking, of doing things. I watched them grow, and as I saw them going in a direction that they shouldn't, I tried to steer them right. Now, did they like it? Sometimes. Other times, no. Just as my parents have been there, done that, so have I.

We won't always get it right; most children want to experience all that life has to offer. But it depends on what you are trying to risk. Again, as a parent, I am not willing to risk my children's salvation if I see they are going down the wrong path. I want my children to trust me enough to know that I won't tell them anything wrong. If I feel this way about my own children, who are also God's children, how much more do you think God feels about his? God knows us from beginning to end. He is a loving Father who gives us grace and mercy.

Little miracles happen every day, and that big miracle you may still be waiting for will come at God's appointed time. Trust him. You must understand that there is a bigger picture. It's about knowing who your source is, and that source is God. He is self-existing. He is the Alpha and the Omega. The tests we go through are meant to strengthen us and give us courage for the mission ahead. I can honestly say that from then until now, I feel so much stronger and braver in my walk with the Lord (I never would have had the courage to write this and my first book if not for him). I know I have come a long way from the shy girl who was afraid to speak up, who struggled with low self-esteem, and who was an easy target for bullies.

God sees me, and he is guiding me through this life. I don't believe that God will leave me after bringing me this far. I have no intention of giving up on him, even though he has carried me through so much. I believe in his promises, and I feel secure in his love for me. God and I alone know what he has spoken over my life. I am standing firmly on the word he has given me. I may look crazy to others, and it may frustrate them more than it frustrates me, but I've learned that I don't need their understanding. I am trusting God to manifest his promises in his time.

It has been a long journey for me; I go back to my journals to read what he has promised and remind myself to hold on because I get weary, I must hang on to hope, I pray for strength all the time, but I remain obedient to my Lord. (In your weak state, you may try to fix things on your own but remain obedient). Even when God is silent, when I don't hear a word, there are moments when I search my heart, wondering if I have done something wrong or if God is displeased with me.

I went from daily encounters with him to what felt like silence, and I questioned what had changed. But I've come to believe that in those quiet seasons, God is inviting me to seek him more deeply, the same way I would seek out a loved one I haven't seen or heard from in a while. He uses those moments to grow our relationship, to stretch my heart, and to teach me to recognize his presence in new ways. It's like the saying, "absence makes the heart grow fonder," a popular phrase by Thomas Haynes Bayly. Not because God is ever truly absent, he is always with us, just as he promised. And God doesn't lie.

I believe the Lord also uses those moments to teach me how to be still, to quiet my spirit so I can truly listen to his voice and align my heart posture towards him. God is infinitely wise, and we are wise when we choose to follow him. He takes us on a journey of renewal, and even when we don't know which way to go, we know this much: we cannot stop walking in the ways of the Lord. God is not the author of confusion, so don't get tangled in fear over what you should or shouldn't do or the decisions you're facing. Trust me, the Holy Spirit will check you when something isn't right. If you ignore his prompting, he will keep bringing it to your attention, pressing it on your heart until you can't find rest, because deep down you already know when something is out of alignment with God's will. The Holy Spirit makes it clear when your walk is not the way of the Lord, and he also gives peace when you are walking in the direction God has called you to follow. Even in relationships.

Obedience is better than sacrifice. Obedience requires faith in the one who sent you, the one who orders your steps, and the one to whom you said "yes". Obedience can be as simple as not eating grapes in a store that you have no intention of purchasing from. Don't do that, be sensitive to the Holy Spirit, prompting you to purchase the grapes, and then eat them, or something as difficult as starting a new business. Did he tell you to do it? If God brought you to it, he's going to bring you through it. That business will flourish when God puts his stamp on it. You know how God does it, he will not be outshone. Overflow. There are so many rewards to being obedient. I depend on him to order my footsteps; to guide me where I need to go. God is always near and ready to answer when we call. If God said he will do it, then I will believe him for it. Trust is a part of the learning process, but we must trust him to take care of us.

Chapter 23 - Difficult Journey

Being saved is easy; it's the journey that can be difficult. Romans 10:9-10 states that confessing Jesus as Lord and believing in His resurrection from the dead leads to salvation. What you must know is that the world doesn't truly embrace your journey with Christ. When you follow Christ, you may lose those whom you called friends, you may lose status, and you may lose the things you hold close. I don't even want to talk about isolation, I mean, everyone except one or two were gone, my phone made its own silent button. No one to talk to about what you are going through because they just don't get it, and you can't explain it. You may say, "What is the benefit then if I lose everything?" Well, you gain eternal life.

Do you believe in heaven or hell? I'm here to tell you that they exist. Your love for the world or your love for Christ will see you in one or the other. I choose Christ; it's a win-win situation. All that I experienced, I don't look like what I have been through, from the inside out, Jesus owns me. What I gain in Christ is everlasting and eternal; this includes what I gain here on earth. Yes, of course, you will have to go through some things, trials and tribulations, but that is true for worldly gain as well. But worldly gains are not as rewarding in the long run; don't be fooled by what it looks like on the surface. They look like they have it all, but they are missing Jesus. What happens when all worldly gain is gone? Some cannot, or are unwilling, to continue living without it. When you don't have Jesus in your life, your spirit is dead, no feeling, no joy, no happiness, etc. (Jesus is everything; the devil is not). Behind the scenes, they are scrambling to make it look good, to make you envious and jealous, and to want the things that they have. All the material things in the world can't get rid of the emptiness on the inside. But they can pretend like it's nobody's business, and it fools lots of people. It's intentional from the enemy.

What God blesses you with, if you continue to follow him, no one can take it away. That includes your soul. What? I give my life to the Lord, and I am saved? Yes, remember, Romans 10:9-10. We are God's children, so he put his stamp on us. Don't be ashamed to claim him either; let the whole world know that you are a child of God wherever you go, whatever you do in life. He will never leave nor forsake us; his word does not return to him void. He keeps his promises. Also, remember Mark 8:36, *"For what shall it profit a man, if he shall gain the whole world, and lose his own soul?"* You only have one soul, so don't sell it to the devil. He is a trickster; he'll make you think that the things of this world will make you happy, or that people will make you happy, and you put your trust and faith in them. Jesus is the only way to God, and what does that mean? You can't buy your way into heaven, nor cheat your way, nor do so much good on this earth that you think God will make an exception. No, believe in Jesus and make him Lord of your life, of course, changes are going to be made once you do.

This world is "chasing a high" that they will never reach; whatever they think they can get to fill the void of emptiness, they will try. Unfortunately, they would be lost. Only Jesus Christ can fill that void with love, joy, peace, happiness, hope, goodness, kindness, long suffering, strength, etc. It's not something that you can go around; you can't work for it, but once you have it, you are safe from eternal death. I'm talking about salvation. It's a must-have.

Chapter 24 - Being Real with God

The journey to faith was very enlightening. This faith thing is no joke, and frankly, it is not to pacify Christians. Faith walk is hardcore, and being lukewarm won't get you past the basics. This has been a deeply personal experience for me. I've learned that real faith isn't about words or appearances; lip service means nothing compared to truly living it. I remember when my son was born, he had pyloric stenosis, and he almost died because he was projectile vomiting so much that he had lost a lot of his electrolytes. The doctors told me that if we had waited one more day, our son would not have made it. That was the worst feeling in the world; no parent wants to hear about the near-death of a child. Of course, we went back and forth to the doctor, changing his formula, and doing whatever we could to fix it, to no avail.

One Sunday, my late husband and I went to the altar at our church, and he called out our son's name for prayer, the next day I was being led to take him to the ER, my husband called home before I dropped the girls off to school to tell me the Holy Spirit was prompting him to let me know to take him to the ER as well. My late husband was a truck driver, and he had left early that morning but said he would turn around if he needed to. My son needed surgery, but his electrolytes needed to be corrected first; they were extremely low. His doctor said that if they sedate him, he may not come out of it. My husband had come back, and we were taking turns spending the night with our son at the hospital, because we still had our daughters to care for.

One day before the young lady drew my son's blood, I prayed over it, and I declared I had an out-of-body experience. I was at the foot of his bed, watching myself pray over my son and that blood work. I was calling on my God, who is our healer. It was a couple of days after I asked for the results that I didn't understand why they waited to give them to me. Everything was good except for the potassium, which could be corrected with a potassium bag. Our son had his surgery on Monday morning at six months old. It was a success, and he is thriving today. Hebrews 11:1 *"Now faith is the substance of things hoped for, the evidence of things not seen"*. We were hoping for a miracle even when everything was very bad. Every day those nurses had nothing but bad news, I really wanted to avoid them because they were bringing me down. Looking at it now, I see the hands of the enemy trying to make me lose hope, lose faith in God.

I don't know what prompted me to pray over that blood at that time, because they were drawing blood all the time. I'm glad that in my obedience, in my hope to grab onto the hem of the Lord's garment, our son was made whole. Thank you, Jesus! If he did it before, he would do it again. The problem is that we forget what God has done for us in the past, what he is doing for us in the present, and what he is already doing for our future. He is omnipresent. So, here is what I am learning. God sends us through tests; at least I am going through tests. Those tests, the enemy exacerbates, have his way with us.

We lose our focus on God because of the raging storm happening in our lives. I had to learn to continue to praise God through the storm, not easy, but we must do it. What the praise does is keep our focus and thoughts on God, because we are submitting to God, acknowledging that we are aligning ourselves with the Lord, and that he is in control, we are resisting the devil's tricks, we are standing with the Lord against evil and the devil flees because we have resisted the temptation to fall, he knows he lost that battle, that's from James 4:7. Read the scriptures, study the scriptures. We must know the word so we can understand what God will do. This is our armor against the enemy. Pray day and night and cover yourself and your loved ones in prayer. The enemy will use anyone to come against you, so stay alert and keep your guard up; he's always lurking. But once we are armed with our weapons for spiritual warfare, the darts the enemy sends will fail. Why? Because you have drawn closer to the Lord, and he has promised to go before you and stand as your defender behind you, Isaiah 52:12; so, you know that he is our protector and that he wants good things for us.

Have faith, even the size of a mustard seed, enough to get you to pass that test and to see the enemy for who he is…A Liar. When your way looks dense, and you can't see your way out, know that Jesus is your light. You must look past the fog and don't be afraid of what is in front of you. *"Walk by faith, not by sight,"* 2 Corinthians 5:7. Take a deep breath, slow down, and talk to the Lord. Listen for his answer, most of the time, at least for me, it was an easy fix. Stop hearing what others are saying; it's the enemy sending you mixed messages. Confusing you. Only listen to the voice of God; he sends positive messages. The enemy brings negative messages; you must learn to discern the truth and rebuke him so that he will flee. Always pray for answers. Quick testimony about having faith: I was talking to this older gentleman who told me he had a hole in the roof of his home.

He had been trying to get someone to fix it, but because it was winter, no one would come out. He was frustrated because he listened to the weather reports saying it would snow or that we would have rain. I told him about the times I asked God not to let it rain until I got to my destination, and he did. I asked him to pray, ask God for the same, and believe that it would happen. That was a couple of months ago.

He came in recently and reported that for five days, his roof was open and not one drop of rain or snow fell, then someone finally fixed it, and he has not had any problems since. He was so happy. He said he listened to me, and it worked. Bless God. My faith in God gets stronger daily, but it still doesn't mean that you won't get discouraged, or that you won't have moments of doubt, we are human and we have human feelings, we get weak, that's why we need God for strength, and don't get me wrong, we still go through things because God still wants to strengthen us for the battles that we fight daily, to give us courage to spread the word of God to the world.

In a world where true Christianity is not popular and itching ears only want to hear about the blessings of the Lord, not what it takes to walk a Christ-centered life. God sent his only son to this world as a perfect example for us to mimic, and that son is Jesus. His journey on earth was 33 years, preaching, teaching, and loving us, preparing us for what's to come. Which is why it is a journey we will walk until the Lord calls us home. I have faith that God will provide for me just like he has been providing for his children since the beginning of time. We are all on different journeys; our tests speak to what is going on in our lives. I still have my late husband's truck. God promised me a new one, but I think I have a lesson to learn about trusting God in this situation and having faith that He will keep me safe, preserve me, and manifest.

There will be new trials and tribulations to overcome. I pray over the truck every day for safe travels and for it to hold up. I am not as anxious about driving it as I was. I'm seeing God in it, that he has me. Even though I don't see anything happening, I have reached the point where I can wait, trust, and have faith in his appointed time. But whenever I pause in my praise or get lax in my prayers, because we do, I start to waver and lose focus. It's not God; he's still the same. I took my eyes off the Lord. I told you, the enemy is always lurking and watching so that he can pounce. We must put on our armor every day and be ready to fight a good fight. When we do, we know that God will always be with us through it all.

Chapter 25 - Out Of Darkness

The journey to finding my savior gave me great joy, but it also revealed some things in my life that I was ashamed of; when the enemy obscures your focus with distractions, you don't even realize that you need saving. I needed saving, I needed a wakeup call because I was headed towards disaster. Yes, that's right, I said it. I was headed towards disaster. Not even realizing that my thoughts could get me in trouble. I didn't know something so innocent could turn dark. I'm talking about romance novels. I enjoy them because I am a romantic at heart.

I was working the night shift, and one of my coworkers noticed me reading and asked what I was reading, so I told her it was a romance novel. Another night, she came over to me and told me about the book "Fifty Shades of Grey." I didn't know what kind of book it was, but I was sold on the romantic part. Then she said, " It's a trilogy, so you have to download all of them. I did it because I hate cliffhangers. I got into the book and read them all. I was very fascinated with them. (You know, I feel like Eve being deceived by the snake because my eyes were opened to a whole new world) I found myself looking for more of that kind. Those books filled the space when things were quiet. I let my imagination flow. I was the heroine in those novels. It gave me a false sense of bravery, as if my sexuality could give me power over a man's heart and mind.

Ephesians 5:8 says, *"For ye were sometimes darkness, but now are you light in the Lord: walk as children of light,"* but I was walking in darkness for sure. You can walk down the wrong path, unaware, and get into some serious trouble. God was truly with me, but I had to see the mistakes I was making so I wouldn't do them again. God was sending me warnings, but I wasn't listening. I remember going to church, and the Holy Spirit made his presence known, but I felt nothing; I couldn't understand what was going on. I felt empty.

As time went by, I slipped into the darker romance novels; I didn't even want to read the lighter books any longer. My thoughts started to go left and were so dark that I thought I wanted that type of life to try it out. I found myself going on the dating site to see if I would attract that type of guy. Wherever I went, I tried to look the part of a submissive woman. I was so drawn in to what I thought were normal desires. Meanwhile, I was going through the motions of church life, and I felt like the Holy Spirit was far away from me. Y'all God hates sin, even the ones in your mind; he can hear them even before you think them. OH, my goodness! That can't be good; my thoughts were not the thoughts of the Lord. I didn't think what I was doing was wrong. I was leaning towards my own understanding. I had a wakeup call when I was taking self -defense classes, it was mixed gender at first, and then it eventually was me being the only female with the guys. I was attracted to one of the instructors. I never said anything to him; I just made myself available by always showing up for class and trying to partner with him during the demonstrations, which allowed us to have close contact.

For a while, it was okay, but then other participants started coming, and some of the moves that were done required them to be between my legs. I was mainly wrestling with men, because, as I said, I became the only female in the class. But I continued to go. The feeling of "wrong" was creeping in, but I stayed. I felt like I was being tested, and I still stayed. One of the newer guys told me I should go to a women's class, and I was thinking, "You can't tell me what to do." I was hardheaded. Yes, I stayed. He approached me again with his girlfriend, whom I was having a conversation with, and he said, “You should go to another class because you don’t want these men all over you like that,” and I stared at him and thought, “Oh my goodness, what have I been doing?” I was being reckless by putting myself in a position to be used. I admit I was very vulnerable and weak at that time in my life. I wanted attention, but sometimes you can attract the wrong attention. I left that day and came back one more time, but I was with a female that time. We were tossing each other, and I landed hard and hurt my back. I never went back. Lesson learned. God said enough.

I think about the me I was three years ago, how that woman wanted to be seen at any cost, and how she thought that being used was how someone should love her. I know that I was lost, I was deep in darkness, and you know what else, I felt like the Holy Spirit was leaving me. I kept saying that I don’t feel right, I felt empty, I was at church and felt only numbness, but Jesus found me and saved me from certain death.

We can’t allow loneliness and fear to determine the path that we take. I had allowed unwanted spirits to enter, but God stopped them from taking over. Thank you, Jesus! Reality checks are in order; Satan is real and is very sneaky.

He attacks our minds at a young age, middle age, or older age; it doesn't matter. His agenda is to kill your ideas, your dreams, steal your innocence, and destroy your life. What seems innocent might not be what it seems; take a closer look. I thank God for hiding me. I wasn't strong and thought I needed someone else's strength to balance me. I was wrong! God saw me, he knew I needed saving, and he was watching over me. God is the only strength that I will ever need.

Nehemiah 8:10 says, *"The joy of the Lord is my strength."* He gives me joy and peace and a love for myself; he has awakened boldness and spiritual power within me. The enemy wanted me to feel unworthy and ugly on the inside; he wanted me to break so that I couldn't rise or be put back together again. Satan is a Liar! I stopped reading romance novels (and don't get me wrong, there is nothing wrong with them; it's how you let them direct your life, as with anything else you do). I replaced them with the word of God and learned how he loves me so much and will fight my battles for me. How he provides for me, protects me, and is reckless for me. I bask in his love daily.

I no longer live for the dark; God drew me to his light and wants to shine his light within me for his glory. The attention that I was seeking, God's got it. He has my attention. That's how I began my journey to becoming born-again saved. It's totally not the same as saying you believe in Jesus Christ and saying you are a Christian, lip service. It is a daily walk, intentional love, and obedience to his commandments, loving your enemies, praying for them, and having brotherly love. It is having joy in your heart and love doing good things for yourself and others. It is waking up, talking to God, and waiting on him to answer (I asked God a question last night and got an answer this morning, but sometimes it takes a few days or more. That's the relationship we have).

It's trusting that he knows the best time to answer you. God doesn't save us to leave us alone in this world, to fend for ourselves. Once he saves us, we must be alert to his guidance and act upon it. He will not play with you or pacify you; we are on his schedule, not ours. So don't think that you are young and have your whole life to get it together. Wrong thinking. Tomorrow is not promised to anyone, and you don't want to leave this world unsaved, because that would be your last chance, no more chances to get Christianity right.

God gives us so many chances to live a Godly life; it's our choice to follow him or not.

John 3:16 says, *"For God so loved the world, that he gave his only begotten Son, that whosoever believeth in him should not perish, but have everlasting life."* Don't waste the greatest gift of all. It's not just believing; it's doing the work, it's sacrificing, it's intentional, it's all the things that he does for us daily. We owe God everything. Don't get me wrong, I still love a good love story. I look for the real love stories that God has put together. I am waiting for my love story that he is working on for me. Good, healthy love that God intended for all his children. His love shows us how we are to be loved and feel safe in a God-ordained marriage. He saves us because he wants the best for us.

Chapter 26 - God My Protector

God, my protector, *"when the enemy comes in like a flood, the spirit of the Lord will raise a standard against him"* Isaiah 59:19. My journey of realizing that God is truly my protector. Satan has been after me for a very long time. What I am noticing is that the times he tries to attack me the most have been in my vehicles, but he attacks whatever I hold dear: my husband, my children, my home, my family, my schooling, my career, etc.

I remember when we lived in Memphis, I was on my way home from work. I usually drive in the slower lane because I am not a fast driver; my family calls me "grandma" on the road. I was in the middle lane and about to move to the right, slower lane, when I heard a loud whisper say, "Don't go!" I looked up in the rear-view mirror and said "huh?" because it sounded like someone was in my car with me. As I was looking up, a car zoomed past me, going so fast like the speed of light. I stared for a second as I realized that I was almost in a fatal crash. I was thanking God for saving me, I still tell that testimony of God's protection, his grace and mercy.

More recently, I was driving in my truck on the expressway in the left lane because I don't like to change lanes, and it took me all the way to my destination. It was windy outside, and suddenly, my hood on the truck flew up. I didn't panic like I normally would; I just slowed down and guided my truck to the shoulder of the expressway and sat until a tow truck came. God was truly with me; no way would I have handled that with the grace that I did. Angels are watching over me.

Another time after that, again on my way to work and my breaks on my truck went out, thank God we were slowed down in traffic, but we were bumper to bumper and I felt something happen, I steered the truck to the shoulder in time before I hit the car in front of me; and was prompted to press on the emergency breaks, I have never pressed the emergency breaks and to know exactly where they were and what to do was God. That would have been a time of panic, and forgetting what to do, but I didn't, and no one hit me while I waited for a tow to get me.

Another time I was on my way home from work, talking to my friend on the phone, I was on the expressway in the middle lane going towards my exit and my hood flew up again, I stopped the truck in traffic, I looked through the opening of the hood and noticed no one was in front of me, but cars were lined up behind me and was going around my truck, I saw the shoulder of the expressway, it was a short distance away, all I needed to do was get over one lane and then to the shoulder but cars would not stop to let me over. (That's how numb and detached the world has become; no one feels the need to help any longer. They just came and went; desensitized) Finally, the car behind me saw her chance and moved her car to block the traffic so that I could ease over to the shoulder. When I was safe, I thanked her. When my truck got to the shop, the mechanic said I was lucky because usually when the hood flies up, it takes the windshield with it. It was God's protection.

The other day, on my way to work at the stoplight, I was about to get on the expressway, and my truck wouldn't make the left turn. I couldn't move it. A good Samaritan saw me and helped me get my truck out of the street, he called a tow truck and told me he owned a shop if I didn't have my own, but I did, so I thanked him for his help. He said it's a good thing that happened before you got on the expressway, morning traffic, people always in a rush… I thank God for his protection.

These were physical things that happened to me, but I am aware that this is a spiritual attack. Some may say buy a new car, and I say donations are always welcome. But that's not the only way that God protects me. He gives me warning dreams. I didn't understand them at first, but God is so wise that he led me to follow someone who would give me a better understanding of how to interpret my dreams. I didn't want to keep dismissing them just because I didn't understand them or what to do about them. The funny thing about dreams: nobody wants you to dream about them, and they don't want you to tell them about the dream. It's almost taboo, lol. When God gives me a dream, I wake up, write it down, and start doing some biblical research.

See, I had to realize that God was talking to me through my dreams. He was giving me all kinds of warning dreams about trouble, rape, bodies of water, family storms, and other things. Some of the dreams are so crazy or extraordinary that at first, I did think it was a pizza dream, but I learned that extraordinary dreams are for us to take notice of them; they stay on the mind, they won't go right away, however, you will start to lose parts of the dream if you don't write it down as soon as you wake up. I had to learn that I shouldn't ignore those dreams but pray over them.

So that's what I started doing. I pray. When he gave me dates, if anyone I knew was doing something on that day, I would fast and pray; he would always confirm what might have happened when that person called me with an "almost" incident. See, dreams are not just for me, but for others as well. I have learned not to share so much unless I feel like the Lord is prompting me to do so. Not all will understand or accept the journey that God has for you, or maybe it's the vessel that God is using that is not understood or accepted. Again, my journey. I am humbled by his trust in me to give me dreams. God is so faithful, he won't just do it for me; He will gift you as well, but you must really seek him. Stay in his word that guides us; it's our map to the right path to our ultimate destination.

Chapter 27 - Healer

The journey to healing was kind of difficult for me. After my husband passed, I was angry, hurt, worried, and scared. I couldn't believe everything that was happening to me. You wouldn't believe how people will take advantage of your vulnerable state. I had to build a wall against everyone because I couldn't trust anyone to help me sincerely. You can't share your plight with everyone because they will pounce like the enemy. The others just sit back and laugh at your struggles. I had to learn to forgive so I could heal. I had to learn to love my enemies regardless of how they treated me. But I also learned how to stand up for myself and stop letting people take advantage of me.

I learned how to negotiate with a tow truck driver, how to look up how to change a washer filter, and how to do lawn care. See, I didn't stay in that defeated state of mind. I didn't allow the enemy to make me crumble. Just because people are miserable and mean-spirited and have no compassion in them, doesn't mean that you should give them room in your head to disrupt your life or peace. Overcome, that's what it is. These were the sort of things my late husband took care of; I didn't have to worry about anything that I considered "man's" work. I felt safe with my husband; he really took care of me, and he was my friend. He was very funny; he made me laugh.

People want to tell me about the younger version of him that I didn't know, because they don't understand that when you meet Jesus, the old you is no more; the new you is what everyone should see. The problem is that people will try to keep you in your past because that's what they are comfortable with, not the growth that they see in you, and sadly, they will not follow you in your growth but will try to pull you down. Don't let that happen.

When God changes you from the filth of your past, it is buried; don't let anyone dig it back up, not even you. Let go of the past and obtain peace. We heal from the things people say about us; words can be very unkind when delivered that way intentionally, even the things people do to us that hurt us deeply. It may seem like you can't move from that space of feeling powerless. Know that Jesus himself has been confronted by obstacles that seemed like nothing could move them. We must know that when Jesus won victory over death, sin, and Satan, we rose with him; we are overcomers. There is nothing too hard for God, Jeremiah

32:27. No sickness, illness, disease of the mind, body, or spirit is too hard for God to heal.

We must do our part in truly believing, not just in circumstantial belief. You know, when it happens to you, the first thing you do is ask God to heal you or them, and because you asked, it should be done, right? So, when it is not done when you think it should, you lose faith in God, and you doubt. Once you start doubting, you are canceling out everything that you believed. We can't get distracted by what we don't see happening before us; hold on. God heals, though sometimes it may not be as you expect.

Did you know that healing is even unto death? I had to learn that when my mother was sick and passed away. We prayed so hard for her to get well, and when she didn't, it was unreal. I remember when my brother spoke those words to us, "healing can be unto death," and it seemed like as soon as I accepted that, my mom died. She was the glue to our family, and as time passed, the glue that held us together started becoming "unstuck". We became that broken family. If there are cracks, if we are torn apart, if we are separated, if we are not together, we are broken, and we are hiding it. Pretending it's not happening doesn't mean we are not broken. Loving each other doesn't mean we don't need fixing.

My mom left a legacy; she taught her husband and children about Jesus Christ, and that we should have a personal relationship with him. See, she followed Christ and knew the importance of us knowing him for ourselves. She knew that she couldn't save us, but she knew how to pray for us and try to steer us in the right direction. Our walk with Christ is our own. My prayer is for us to wake up, allow God to open our eyes and ears to hear from him.

Over time, I began to learn about personal relationships with our Lord. Jesus is our true glue, and slowly, he is bringing us back together. I continue to pray for healing in my family, that we are restored to even better than we were when my mom was here. The distractions of life, the paths that we take, should only be lessons learned; they shouldn't cause us to harbor any animosity, hatred, or jealousy of our loved ones. I hope we realize that we serve the same God who can bless all.

The enemy causes chaos in families; we must know this, that we are dealing with spiritual things in high places whose mission is to destroy families by causing friction, but God will turn it around; that's why we pray in season and out of season. Just like the father of the prodigal son in Luke 15:11-32, who welcomed his son back with open arms and forgave him, we know that forgiving is healing for ourselves and restorative. It can open hearts to not being so selfish in our ways, in the way we treat each other or dismiss one another. Through the grace of God, it can bring family and friends together in healthy and healed relationships.

Chapter 28 - Inward Change

The Good Lord must clean us up, mentally, spiritually, and physically. Outward showing of an inward change. I think it's a lifetime process. I had a recent encounter with someone. We were discussing my walk with Christ, and I was telling him how I used to be a surface Christian with a surface-level understanding and belief. When I shared some of my experiences with him about how much deeper it is to walk with God, and how he had to purge me, refine me, and get me ready for my calling. He stopped me and held out his hand to say, "Maybe I don't want to go deeper," but I told him that once you truly know God, you will want to know more.

We can't be afraid of the unknown and stay in what we think is our safe haven. The enemy knows that fear will stop us from doing what God has set for us to do. But also know that when God comes after you, when he chases you, you will come, willing or kicking and screaming, because he knows you can handle it, he knows what is best for you, just ask Saul on that road to Damascus when he encountered Jesus, and was changed from Saul to Paul, Acts 9. That's just who our God is; he is Sovereign and All-Knowing. His plan for our lives is not to harm us, but to prosper us. Fear keeps that from happening, so he gives us a little push in the right direction. We are worthy of the calling that God has on our lives. Don't be afraid to walk into your destiny. Don't feel guilty that God put you there; you went through the fire! You deserve it, so no shame in what you experienced, you overcame it, and now you testify about what God has brought you through and to.

Some of the things that we went through and thought were buried have a way of resurrecting. Yeah, I'm talking about hidden deep, blocking it out of your mind, not even in conversations do you remember it. But, for God to make us ready for what he is calling us to do, that secret must be revealed. Why Lord? I thought this was between you and me. I thought if I asked for forgiveness with a sincere heart, it would stay buried. I thought it would be cast into the sea of forgetfulness, so I forgot about it, too. Apparently, that is not the case. For us to heal and be made whole, we must come clean with all those things that keep us bound. Secrets. (Because the enemy dwells in darkness, secrets are darkness, and you can't overcome them if they are buried). Now I'm not telling you to bear all your secrets; if the Lord isn't asking you to resurrect them, then put the shovel down. Don't take it upon yourself to do something that might affect many people, so pray about it first.

Testimonies are to help others who are going through similar situations and need to know that there is a way out if you trust God to guide you through it. It is by no means meant to shame you or for others to hold you bound by their gossip. Overcomers! So, what I am about to share, I'm not sure if it's a testimony because I'm not sure why God wants me to speak on it. I cried so many tears over this when it happened, and during, I asked God for forgiveness and then buried it deep, so much so that it was like a slap in the face when it came to the forefront of my mind. It wouldn't leave me, I cried again, in my bed, because I wanted to know why a need for me is there to bring back what I had buried? Because God doesn't want me to be shackled to what was my shame, he doesn't want me to fear what people would say. He wants others to know the same.

He knows how people are, mean-spirited gossipers, and nasty with words. How they judge: Matthew 7:1-2 says, *"Judge not lest you be judged."* God also said, "*Be strong and of a good courage, fear not, nor be afraid of them; for the Lord thy God, he it is that doth go with thee; he will not fail thee, nor forsake thee*," Deuteronomy 31:6. God is my champion, my hero. He goes before me and is a defender behind me! So, I decided to continue in my obedience to my Lord and share because I am not afraid of what people say. No heaven or hell to place you or me in. People are unforgiving until it is them who need forgiving, but do we shackle ourselves down with guilt, shame, and defeat so that others can feel good about themselves? Or, and I believe this is true for me.

People perceive me in a certain way; they think that because I am quiet, I must be more than others, and they judge me before getting to know me. They dismiss me, overlook me, and believe me to be the person that they want to hate. I am by no means perfect, but I am perfectly made by my Lord. It's the light of Jesus Christ shining within me that they hate. I had to learn that over the years. My faith walk has not been easy. I have made so many mistakes and wrong choices. But God is ever faithful, loving, and forgiving. Thank God he is not a man!

Here we go, first let me begin by saying that I had a child out of wedlock; actually, I had two, and when I met my husband, he was separated from his wife but not yet divorced.

The Lord separated us for five years; we lived in two different states. Around that time, I was approximately 26 and had recently had my second child, who was less than a year old, and my boyfriend at the time (who later became my husband) had found out I was pregnant again. All kinds of thoughts ran through my mind; shame was most prominent. What will my family say? What will my coworkers say? Everyone will talk about me. I did not want to be that girl with a whole lot of children and was unmarried. I had no thoughts about the life growing inside me.

Psalm 51:5 says, *"Behold, I was shaped in iniquity; and in sin did my mother conceive me."* Sin, unfortunately, is a human quality that is present in every human being, even at conception. And I wasn't exempt from it, again, not perfect. I was already told that I would have children before I graduated high school, but I didn't; I graduated as a virgin. College was not an option for me at the time, so I went to trade school and graduated. I landed a job with a small clinic, even though the interview was tragic. God was ordering my steps, but I didn't know it. I was still making my own decisions. I was a quiet, shy girl, extremely so. I wasn't outgoing or brave. I know now that the Lord was leading me through life, and how did I repay him? I aborted the life that he gave me. There was no excuse for such an act. That was the worst day of my life. That was the first and the last time I ever visited an abortion clinic. I cried and prayed during the whole process; I was alone and scared and ashamed. When it was over, I started to laugh and cry uncontrollably. I don't know why I did it. I was in a daze for a while. It hurts that I failed my Lord. I told no one, even after all these years. I blocked the whole experience.

For a while, my head was bowed, I didn't feel like my prayers would be answered, I was afraid to really talk to God, afraid of his rejection. So, I avoided him as much as possible, but he stayed with me. At first, I allowed the guilt to consume me as punishment. I wondered if the baby was a girl or a boy. I used to shut my mouth when the subject of abortions was spoken around me, because I didn't feel like I had a right to speak about it. Those are the tricks of Satan, so that you won't talk someone else out of doing it or any sin. Through the word of God, I learned that God forgave me after I asked for forgiveness and repented. As I said, I never did that again. I am an overcomer; I am free and whole because of the blood of Jesus. Satan is a liar. I am not bound; the chains are broken in Jesus' name!

I cast out any generational curses! Strong holds! Bondages! That may come against my bloodlines, in Jesus' name. Satan won't shut my mouth on speaking what is right and pleasing in the sight of God. Ultimately, it is your choice, and you must deal with the consequences as I have. *"Hide thy face from my sins and blot out all mine iniquities. Create in me a clean heart, O God; and renew a right spirit within me,"* Psalm 51:9-10. God has forgiven me because he is Faithful and just to do so. I speak plainly when I say, "I am not looking for man's forgiveness, man's approval, man's anything." My peace was made with Jesus alone.

Again, I have no idea why he wanted me to share this, but I have, and I hope it reaches the person it is supposed to reach and does what God has moved it to do. Because so many have gone through similar situations and thought that they were condemned to hell. That is not so; Satan wants us to think that there is no way God will forgive us. We may let God down every day, intentionally and unintentionally. It doesn't mean that the enemy has a right to hold it over us. To place a handcuff on us so we can't do the work of the Lord. He accuses us daily before the Lord; he goes to him to tell him what we have done, the devil! Like he has room to talk. (He does to us what we do to each other: point fingers, judge, persecute, blame, hate, and tear down). I feel freer by sharing this, so maybe the Lord wants others not to be afraid of people's opinions or to be bound. Because that's all it is, their opinion. I don't know your circumstances; I don't know why you made your choice. What I do know is that the opinions of others can't supersede the calling that God has on our lives. It gets better day by day. We get stronger day by day. We choose to follow Christ intentionally day by day. No, the journey is not easy, but it is right. Your reward will be greater later; just stay the course.

Shame

You meant to shame me
You laugh at my situation
You mean to offend
You believe I am defeated
So, you whisper to your friends
You judge me because you believe I deserve it
But there is no guilt,
Nor any shame with my father, who adores
He loves me without judging me
He loves me evermore
He chastens me when I do wrong
And sometimes blessings are prolonged
None of it is to my shame
But ultimately for my gain
I wait upon the Lord,
He won’t humiliate
My present struggles won’t last always
Shame is not my fate
My head is lifted; it is held high
That is the promise of El Shaddai
Looking past the situation
And focusing on God
Delivered from the guilt and shame

Countenance unmarred.

Chapter 29 - Finish It

Our journey is not complete; God has much work for us to do here on this earth. Don't be afraid to walk into your destiny. Remember, this is not a destination; we have a continuous job to do until the return of our Lord. We are fighting a spiritual war, and the devil thinks he is winning. He doesn't play fair but try not to focus on what he is presenting before you; most of it is hype anyway, and you won't know it is hype if you react immediately without seeking God to calm the situation. If you focus on what you are seeing, you can't see God. He made promises; you will know what he promised if you read and study his words. (Hint, hint). Get familiar with it; it's your weapon against the enemy.

There is so much chaos in the world, people are confused and can't tell the truth from a lie. The trust factor is no longer something that you have with someone as close as a family member, let alone anyone else. People are hurting, hurting from life, from situations and circumstances, and from the consequences of decisions. Trials and tribulations will come; that is a reality for everyone. But when you place your trust in the Lord, he keeps you. The storm may still come, but it will not be as severe as it is for someone who does not know him. As difficult as my own storm was, I know it was not as bad as it could have been, and that is because I am walking in His Word daily. I am learning who he is, learning how to trust him, and learning to lean on him. I am discovering how he protects me, how deeply he loves me, and how he is for me and desires for me to win. You cannot truly know these things if you do not know him, and how can you know him if you are not reading and studying his Word?

He walks with you daily. He shows you the way if you are willing to listen. He teaches, guides, strengthens, and encourages you to step out in faith. When I wrote my first poetry book, I was led by the Holy Spirit to do it. I found myself writing poetry to calm my spirit, putting into words how I was feeling about the whirlwind of problems hitting my life. When God spoke to me about things I needed to change, the process was not easy. Transformation rarely is. It required obedience, reflection, and intentional study to fully understand what he was saying to me.

For example, he gave me the word "committed". I knew what that word meant in general, but I needed to understand what commitment looked like through God's eyes and how he wanted me to live it out in my own life. That is how he has been guiding my transformation, patiently and purposefully leading me from a caterpillar into a butterfly, and into the woman he created me to be. (Let God transform you into a new person by changing the way you think, Romans 12:2) I'm ready to work.

Life is good in Jesus Christ. I can speak about that because I am living it. Of course, I go through the daily battlegrounds with my spiritual weapons. I'm praying every day, all day, because Satan is at it all day. He tries to deceive people by having them think that God doesn't have to be in every aspect of your life. That's another lie of the enemy! The deception starts with what you think; let God renew your mind. Do not exclude God from anything in your life, your business, your marriage, your children, your church, your hobby, your school, your decisions, your home, your car, your furniture, your health, etc. God makes everything run more smoothly.

Don't separate him from anything in your life. Trust me, it may not go as you think. Sure, he can make changes that may not be what you want, but remember God knows our end from our beginning. He sees what we don't. The journey will be worth it if we do not faint. If we don't give up. Do you believe that God can do this? Do you doubt it? Do you have to see it before you believe it? "*Blessed are they who have not seen and yet have believed"* John 20:29. Have faith, just because you are tired of waiting, doesn't mean God will not keep his promise to you. I believe this may be the main reason people leave the faith. I may be wrong, but people don't have the patience to wait on God, so they lose faith in him, and some will even go to another faith altogether or become an atheist. It's safer than being let down, disappointed, or just tired of fighting for something that you don't know is real because you can't see him. *"O ye of little faith,"* Matthew 8:26. You don't trust the power or the presence of God. You allow your fear and anxiety to rule and make your decisions. You're hurt and angry at God because you decided your own path instead of standing strong and waiting on the Lord to answer your prayers. And you know, he blesses us daily; the small things count too. It may not be the thing that will bring us out of our current situation, but I see for myself how he continues to provide for me, and at the same time, he is teaching me.

Listen, in your faith walk, you must “know” that God is real. Don’t let the enemy persuade you to falter in your faith. Be persuaded that nothing can separate you from the love of God.

Chapter 30 - It's Only the Beginning

Your journey does not end when God manifests what he has promised you. It's not over, I repeat, it is destiny, not a destination, and we have work to do. You have a legacy to pass on for generations to come. It does not end with you or me. We must fight on. The enemy is attacking God's people, beating them down, giving them no hope, no courage, feelings of defeat, and then putting anger and envy in the heart towards those who weathered the storm and came out victorious.

When my journey began, I thought, " Let me get through this storm so I can go back to the way things were." I just wanted normalcy again. I learned that's not the case, and it makes sense. Why would I take off the armor that is keeping me safe from the attacks of the enemy? Why would I stop praying, praising, and being obedient to him? It would defeat the purpose because that's what we were created to do. I have mentioned several times that I am strong and courageous. I could not have made it through my storm if it had not been for God showing up strong in my life.

I'm still standing. I don't want to repeat processes, nor do I want to go back to the way things were. God is taking me and you to another level of his glory, and believe me, new levels, new devils. My goal is to stay in his presence, you know, "seeking him first," where all my blessings flow. I'm not trying to fix what is not broken. Amen.

The Good Lord and I have a plan; he directs, and I follow, and everything is good. Where he is leading me, I don't know; what I do know is that he won't steer me wrong; I trust him to take care of me. He has been preparing me and you for his purpose; don't give up now. And let me say this as well, the work that we do is not for vain glory. You may never get acknowledged for the things you do for the Kingdom of God, but we can't get weary in our work. You may look around and find no one there to help you. It's discouraging, I know, believe me, I know. I have wanted to give up so many times through the years, but God won't let me. I must mount up on wings and soar, keep it moving, because the devil doesn't stop.

I can't get tired, and neither can you. Not even when the blessings are flowing. Don't stop now that you have received what God had for you. We have souls to bring to

Christ, and God has chosen us to do it. Put on your whole armor and be ready to fight, to serve, to be bold for the battle that is already happening in the spirit. We love God, we know that God loves us, so we love his people; that's how we are recognized, by the love we exhibit daily. If we love God, we must feed his people the word of God. His desire must be our desire: to see his people saved from the punishment of sin. Listen, victory is already won.

Exodus 14:14 says, *"The Lord will fight for you, and you will hold your peace."* God is fighting for us; you need to be in the posture of prayer and praise. He has us covered because he is sending us to spread his word, and if God is for us, who can be against us? God cares about your legacy, so embrace your training, embrace your surrender, and embrace your calling. It will be worth it.

Let me tell you about a time when I was a new nurse and working in the ICU for the first time. For some reason, I didn't get much support with acclimating to how you got your promotions. One day, I was in the unit with an older nurse, just the two of us, and she asked me if I was on any committees and on the rapid response team (RRT). She let me know I would need those for any promotions, so I joined a committee and the RRT. When it was time to do my self-assessment, I added those to it. My proficiency was due, and I submitted it. Let me tell you how God works. When it was time for my one-on-one with my manager, she had already given me what she wanted to, but God had turned it around. My immediate manager called me into her office to review my proficiency, and she already explained that I should ignore all the red ink on the papers because her boss had made some adjustments. I had no idea what she was talking about until she showed me my proficiency, and yes, it was full of red ink, but it wasn't bad for me; it was correcting what she tried to give me, which was a satisfactory score. She then told me that her boss, who was the director of nursing, told her I was doing too much for her to give me only satisfactory, so her boss gave me an outstanding score, which led to my first bonus. Hallelujah! God will fight our battles for us, and we don't have to lift a hand. I prayed over my proficiency before I submitted it because I knew my manager wasn't too fond of me.

The previous year, she had given me a satisfactory score, and God showed me that she was doing it again, but also that he was intervening for his daughter. People may have feelings about you that you can't control. It's about you, but has nothing to do with you. It’s the light that they see within you, and they can’t stand it. But they will get over it and get used to it because God loves showing out.

Chapter 31 - In Obedience

Obedience will get you very far. God will keep you out of so many situations if you listen. Keep your face turned towards him. He will also bless you and all you hold dear, beyond anything that you can imagine. The blessings that God has in store for you who follow him and keep his commandments will exceed your imagination. Your needs will be met, even the things you didn't know you needed. Don't be afraid of newness or change; God will make all things new. Receive it.

God can do the impossible; stop looking at things through carnal, human eyes. See through the eyes of God, the impossible things that you believe will never happen; God will make them possible. Your unbelief makes you doubt God's ability to do unbelievable things. So, you don't pray about it because you have unconsciously given up on people, things, or situations, but the God I serve can change anyone, just as he changed Saul to Paul, Hallelujah, traded in the old car for a brand-new car, your situation no longer is a situation but a victory in Jesus' name. God won't fail; we do when we stop believing. (You may wait, and yes, waiting is hard; I speak from experience. He said to pray and believe, and we shall receive it. Prayer changes things, no matter how impossible we believe it to be. Just keep praying until something happens. These are true words; you can't pray one or two times and give up because the devil is tenacious. You must be just as vigilant in your pursuit of the Lord over every person, situation, or thing.

Don't give up on God. I said it before, I'll say it again, God is for us, not against us; he wants his children to win. Believe me when I say the enemy is always looking to see how he can destroy your life. God strengthens us to make it to the other side; life is more than what this world offers. Your soul has an eternal place that it needs to be. The temptations of life, if you succumb to them and don't turn away from them, can determine your destination.

Chapter 32 - You Are Chosen

Right here is where I want you to acknowledge that you are somebody to be seen. You are chosen. God has gifted you with his anointing. You may feel like you are caged in from being able to release your gifts. You have so much to give and yet are unable to be fulfilled because envy blocks your path everywhere you turn; doors are shut, you are ignored because they close their eyes to your talents, your gifts, but it's only because they see the light shining within you. It's bursting through because you continue to persevere. Don't let the devil stop what God has put in you. They may think you deserve their leftovers, but God has a table prepared for you with main courses plus dessert! So, celebrate yourself, clap for yourself, don't look for others to lift you up. People don't want to hear about your journey, the path that you had to take to get to where you are. They only listen to see what they can carry back to others to make them laugh.

Look, you are not going to make everyone happy; that is not your job. Only God can do that. I don't care what relationship you are in; you can't make people happy, love you, or even like you. Sometimes people just want to wallow in misery, and if that is the path that they choose to take, let them. But don't let them take your peace and joy, because the miserable love their parties. When you walk into their vicinity, it is so dark that your light is uncomfortable, and you just want to get out. Do that, and do not take it personally; you must develop tough skin.

Predators look for weakness, ie, Satan, they try to make you question yourself, or doubt yourself, or have negative thoughts about your life. They aim to break you down so that they can feel good about themselves for a moment, and it may very well be the highlight of their life, so give them that. Give them that brief but sad empty gloat because you're about to feast at that table. Continue to step into your open heaven. Receive the favor of the Lord. That's your victory. Hallelujah.

Now, I know I keep talking about the waiting-and-obedience journey, but have you ever known God to be impulsive? Don't get me wrong, God can move quickly for his children, and he absolutely does. But he also wants us to learn, to grow stronger and wiser. Why? Because this journey can be tricky. We must be built up in the word of God so we can resist being swayed or torn down by the enemy, and so we can steward and keep the blessing he gives us. Reality check, the enemy will come after you in the form of family, friends, coworkers, in the church, it doesn't matter. When they see how God is blessing you, when they see his light shining within you, they will be jealous and envious of you. But they don't want to go through what you have been through to get the same. They don't want the journey, just the promise.

Don't let the thought of trials and tribulations stop you from following God. In this life, you will have them; your choice is whether to have God with you or not. If you follow right, you will be changed; no doubt, your haters will be the first to know besides you. Lol. So, when you say that you have learned, you will show God that you have indeed learned it, because a test is coming. I told you; God knows the heart.

God wants our hearts to be more like his: loving, kind, compassionate, forgiving, merciful, etc. he knows when we are ready. Let him do a great work in your life. Remember, the trials and tribulations are to strengthen you, encourage you, and to teach you. Strength comes in many forms, and you never know which one you'll need until that moment calls for it.

Sometimes it's courage that carries you through your hardships. It isn't easy being strong for yourself or for others. We face obstacles every day that require resilience, because life can be cruel and relentless when it tries to break us down. Trials and tribulations come to take us out, and we must decide whether we'll sit back and let it happen or rise and fight. I choose to fight. I refuse to let the enemy claim victory over my life. And once that decision is made to not roll over, to not give up, God steps in and supplies the strength and courage we need to become the overcomers we were always meant to be.

I had the opportunity to witness a woman I worked with battle cancer. She shared honest updates throughout her journey, and I'll admit there were moments when I didn't think she would make it. Cancer so often can feel like a death sentence. She is a small woman in stature, but she showed us all that she had a big heart, a strong spirit, unshakable strength, and incredible determination. It was truly inspiring. After some time, she returned to work in the very same position and is doing well. Her story is a reminder that God can do all things. Although our journeys look different, the need is the same. We all need God's strength and courage to make it through difficult seasons. God is here for us whether we believe in him or not. He is merciful and gracious to us all because he loves us. And he knows exactly what he needs to do in each of our lives. So, stop running and stop fighting alone.

Envy

Why do you want what she has?
Your heart desires what the Lord inspired in her
You want to possess; you want to hold what you think will win
The word is ENVY. Do you know it is a sin?
Negative emotions won't carry you higher
Using your God-given skills will lead to your desires
She can't carry you, and herself too
Her walk is different; she chose the straight, narrow path
Is it fair for her to walk into your envy, into your wrath?
Her walk is to inspire others to do the same
All that she does, she does in Jesus' name
Most will walk and go halfway through
Stop and turn around, because IT JUST WON'T DO!
You envy her perseverance
You envy her standing still
You envy her walk with God
To do His perfect will
His light shines within her
She can't blame you for wanting the same
So, walk the walk, but stay in your lane
And set your envy free.

Chapter 33 - Praise Report!

Praise report! I woke up, getting ready to go to work. I started my truck to warm it up, got in, and noticed the radio wasn't on. I thought my heat was off as well. I was like, "Lord, what's going on, are you trying to tell me something?" and that question stayed on my mind, all the way to work, I was talking to God. Remember, how you respond makes a big difference. You don't want to respond with a negative attitude, because it might not go as you think. I decided to fast that day because I needed a word from him, and he usually answers me when I fast. I'm still in my car, and God reminded me of what he told me about where to get my car, but, like most people, I was waiting on the Lord to do the miraculous and make it happen without me doing my part. I also want to note that God has an appointed time for things to happen, and I believe this was my time.

We can try to do things prematurely, and it might not work out in our favor. In my experience, it didn't work for me previously. I still had learning to do. But God, in his compassion for me, has set my time before me. So, I told you that I was fasting because I needed to know if this was God. I asked for confirmation of any kind, and he gave it to me. I was watching YouTube and came across a YouTuber I follow who spoke about keeping it moving, not just sitting and waiting for God to do everything. She said more, but that's what confirmed it for me. God is so amazing, how he hears and answers prayers. I pulled up the dealership online and started searching for vehicles. I found some that I am going to view. I continued to fast and to trust what God was saying to me, and you already know the enemy was trying to sow doubt in my mind by questioning the purchase process. I rebuked him every time he tried, because God said to trust, not doubt. I wasn't trying to be delayed in getting a new vehicle, lol.

So, the day came, I got up early and went into prayer and thanksgiving. I waited for my dad to pick up my son and me, and we headed over to the dealership. I told my dad where we were going when we got in the car because I didn't want anything sabotaging it. When we got there, I presented the sales attendant with the cars that I wanted to see. He said he had all but one. We went out and looked at all the cars, which were nice, but nothing connected with me until I got to the last car. I started it up, and the radio station was tuned to 93.9. That station appeared in my dream, and I had asked God what it meant and got my answer today. God is so good!

So, you already know that it was the vehicle that I got. God's hands were all over that.

Listen, I went to the dealership for the type of car they sold. God gave me a totally different vehicle, sitting alone among friends, just waiting for me to choose it. My dad told me to get the CarFax for the vehicle, and when we received it, it showed one owner, no accidents, it was well maintained, and it looked great. I let the sales attendant know that I needed to go to my credit union. I went there to get a loan, but they didn't have enough staff, and I was told I wouldn't get it done the same day. I felt an urgency to get this done that day. The banker wanted me to come back Monday or Tuesday, but you know, when God opens a door, you must walk on through it. I felt as if I didn't get it that day, it would no longer be available to me, so I just asked for a cashier's check for the amount. I got it and took it to the dealership, and purchased my vehicle.

The good Lord was honoring my request not to have a note to pay. I thought it would be an all-day process, but it only took three hours to complete. When God does something, it doesn't take long. He aligns us to receive what he has for us, so don't miss it. Listening to the Holy Spirit's prompting led me to my blessing. God placed that vehicle right where he wanted me to find it. Thank you, Lord! It's not hard to follow God; it's only hard when you make it a challenge. We think that God doesn't hear us when we pray, that he doesn't see what we are going through, but Matthew 10:29-31 states, *"are not two sparrows sold for a penny? And not one of them will fall to the ground apart from your father. But even the hairs of your head are all numbered. Fear not, therefore; you are of more value than many sparrows."* He will redeem you.

Chapter 34 - Spiritually Developing

Please remember, your journey is your own, your spiritual growth is yours personally. We are not all on the same level. As you receive the word of God, as seeds are planted and watered, you will start to grow gradually and truly begin to develop a strong relationship with our King. We must also remember that salvation is not just for us; we must plant seeds everywhere we go. The world needs to hear the words of God so that they will receive him as Lord of their life.

God doesn't want anyone to die an eternal death. So, our mission is to spread the word of God to all nations so that all can be saved. Let us all grow in grace and in God's holy principles. Allow God to transform our lives to become who he sees in us, that means to surrender, that means obedience, it means being happy and having joy no matter what is going on in your life. The joy of the Lord is truly my strength. Right now, in my life, my storms are at a distance, wow, that's how God does it, when you grow and understand who he is; you know what he will do for you when you seek him (Satan is still busy, so don't relax.) That's the peace that surpasses all understanding.

I have peace, I don't understand how, because my circumstances have not changed much. Don't get me wrong, he blessed me with a new car, my son was blessed with a job during break, my friend's husband got a job when all hope was lost, and so many other things. But just because my circumstances haven't changed has nothing to do with the fact that God is still reigning high in my life. He doesn't always show us the whole picture at once; he reveals things as we grow in him. He is guiding me, and he will do the same for you if you follow.

Chapter 35 - Stay Strong, Stay Focused!

Life's journeys can be tough at times; it can be a battle to walk the straight path because so many distractions hinder us from staying focused on the goal: Heaven. There will be seasons in which the Lord will require a lot from us, we may feel like we can't take it and want to bail out. We have choices in life, we make choices in the life we live, and how we continue to live is what will make the difference. Please don't allow what you see happening before you to influence the choices you make. Think about what you are about to do before you do it and pray for guidance.

I want to encourage you to have a positive attitude even in the midst of your storm, because God will bring you through it just as he has done for me. Don't give up on God. I told you, he is for us, not against us. So, don't hate the process; it will be worth your time and patience in the end. Stay focused, stay the course. I know it's hard when you don't see anything happening, but you can do it! God is aligning you for greater. If you are feeling shame for your sin, repent and return to the presence of God. He will start to unclog your mind so that he can put ideas there when you align yourself with him. Make yourself available to him and get excited. Put your hands in the hands of the one who can.

Being uncomfortable is okay, just don't let it turn into fear of moving forward. You can resist a lot of things, just don't resist God. The world would be so much better in the hands of our Lord. Follow the course that he is leading you and watch how he blesses you. We must do our part to represent him well. That means we live our lives to please the Lord, not anyone else. Just like Jesus influenced us by how he lived, we must influence others by how we live. Don't have a dirty house and invite others in to dwell in it. Clean it up and present yourselves before the Lord. Don't be discouraged if you don't get everybody to come to the Lord; not all will come, but don't give up. Keep trying. It's our mission from the Lord.

So, my fellow travelers, travel your journey well, you never know who is watching, who needs encouragement, who needs to see your strength. You have strength and hope through Jesus Christ, so make sure to take him with you wherever you travel. The enemy is on that road to distract you into turning away; to go in a different direction from where the Lord is leading you. The enemy won't stop bothering you; he wants you to go where he is going. So, if you stop following Christ, that possibility is strong. I believe in you. If God chose you, then take that baton and run towards your purpose.

God bless you during your process and on your journey of becoming who God sees in you. And remember to have faith in the Only Wise God, and that Jesus is the only way to our Heavenly Father.

YOU WAITED

You waited for us
To come to your light
You waited for us
To gain spiritual sight
We were lost among the sea of brothers.
Born in sin through flesh, through mothers
You patiently wait
For us to hear
The voice of truth
So, you can draw near
It's not your will that we should perish
You waited for us
And we should cherish
The patience of our Loving Father
Who waits to give us a chance
To see him face-to-face
In his eternal resting place.
Question…
What if God didn't wait?

Peace and Blessings.

About The Author

Diana Allen is a Registered Nurse in the Chicago area, the author of "Guiding Light to My Journey". Her writing is deeply rooted in her Christian faith and reflects her belief in the power of faith, family, and community. Diana is an active member of her church, where she serves as the program director of their youth ministry and compassion ministry. Her passion for storytelling is inspired by her desire to uplift, encourage, and share hope through her words.

In her downtime, she enjoys reading and writing, finding peace and inspiration in quiet moments. She is deeply committed to guiding and inspiring the next generation.

Connect with Diana

Email – authordianaallen@gmail.com

www.ingramcontent.com/pod-product-compliance
Lightning Source LLC
LaVergne TN
LVHW010618100826
845148LV00014B/3016

* 9 7 9 8 9 8 6 4 5 9 5 4 7 *